Tsukiji

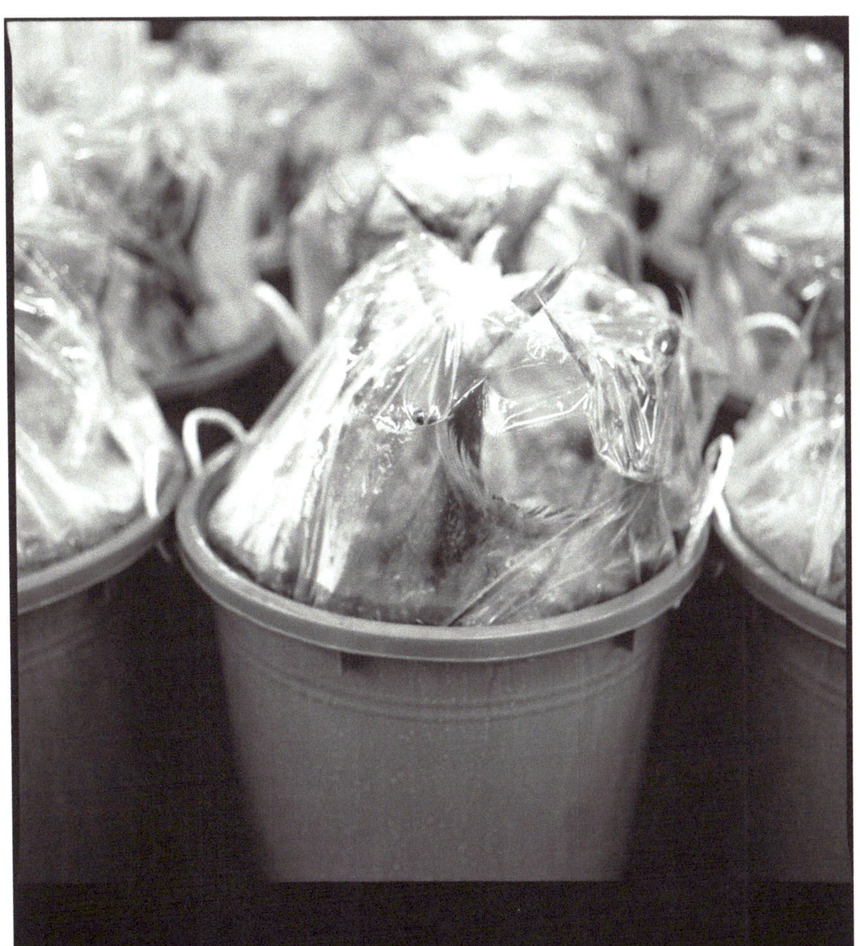

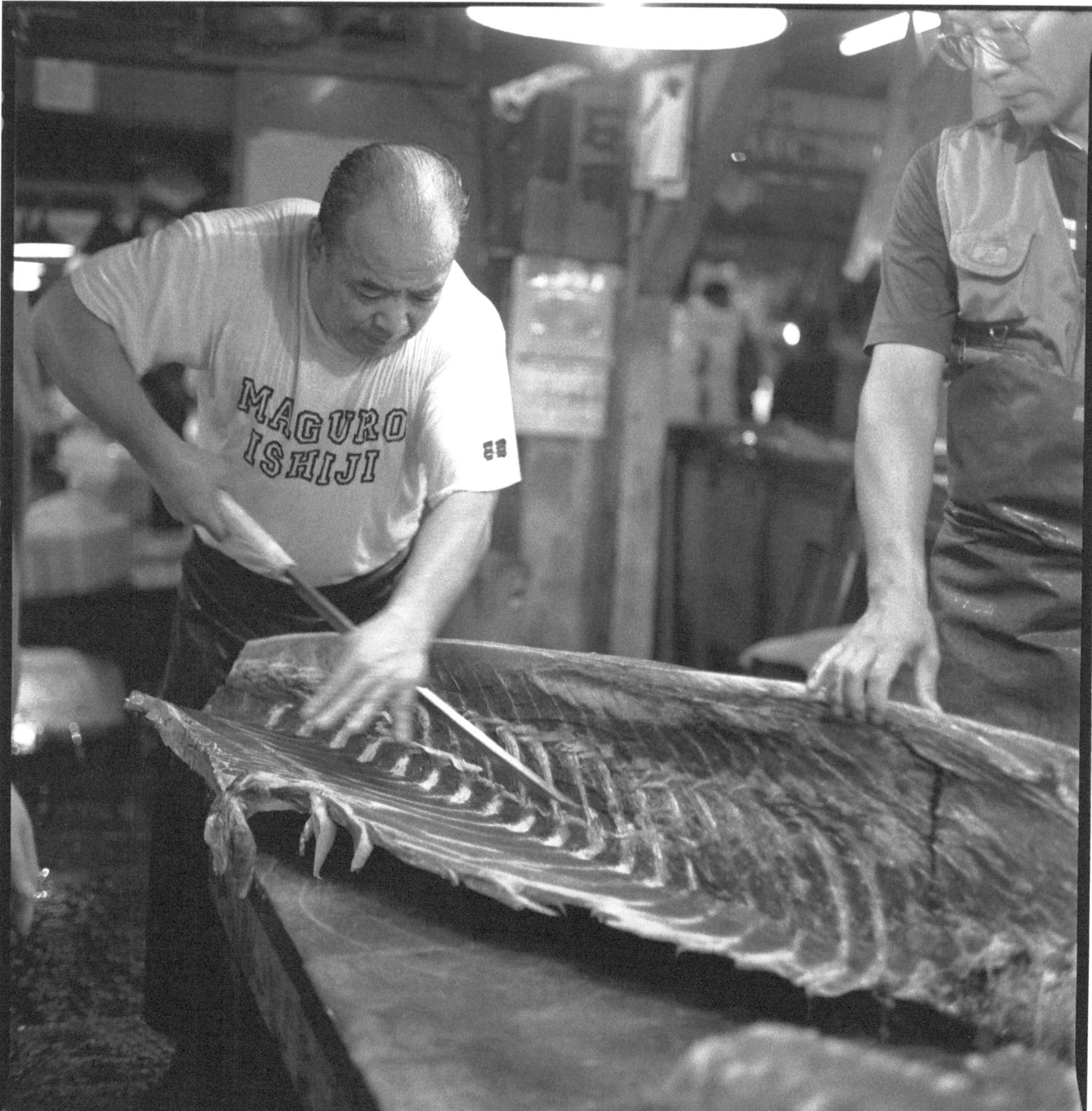

MAGURO
ISHIJI

Tsukiji

William Ash

Tokyo Fish Market Suite

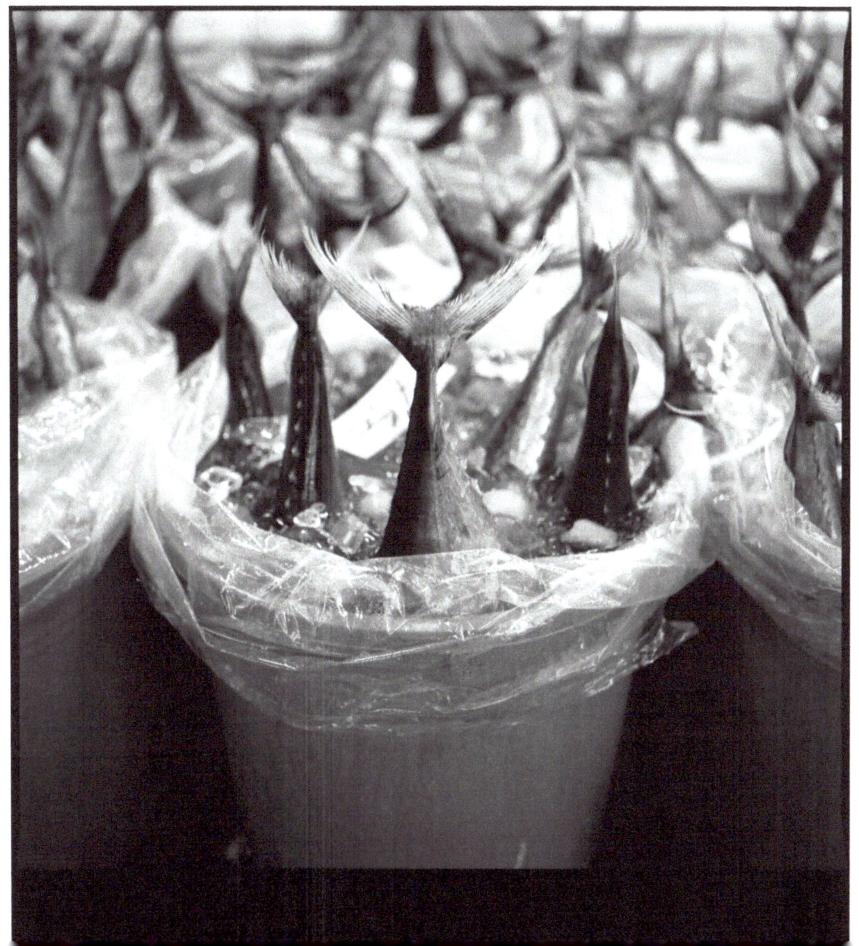

Tsukiji: Tokyo Fish Market Suite

Hakusan Creation
www.hakusancreation.com

ISBN: 978-1-935461-10-4

Printed in the United States of America

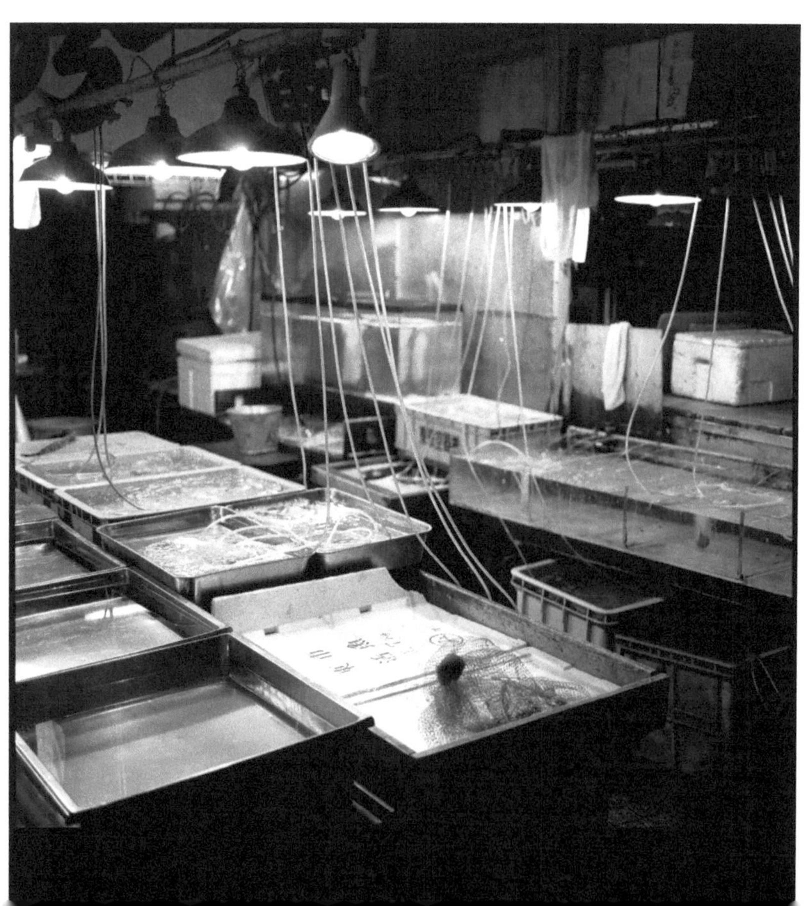

Contents

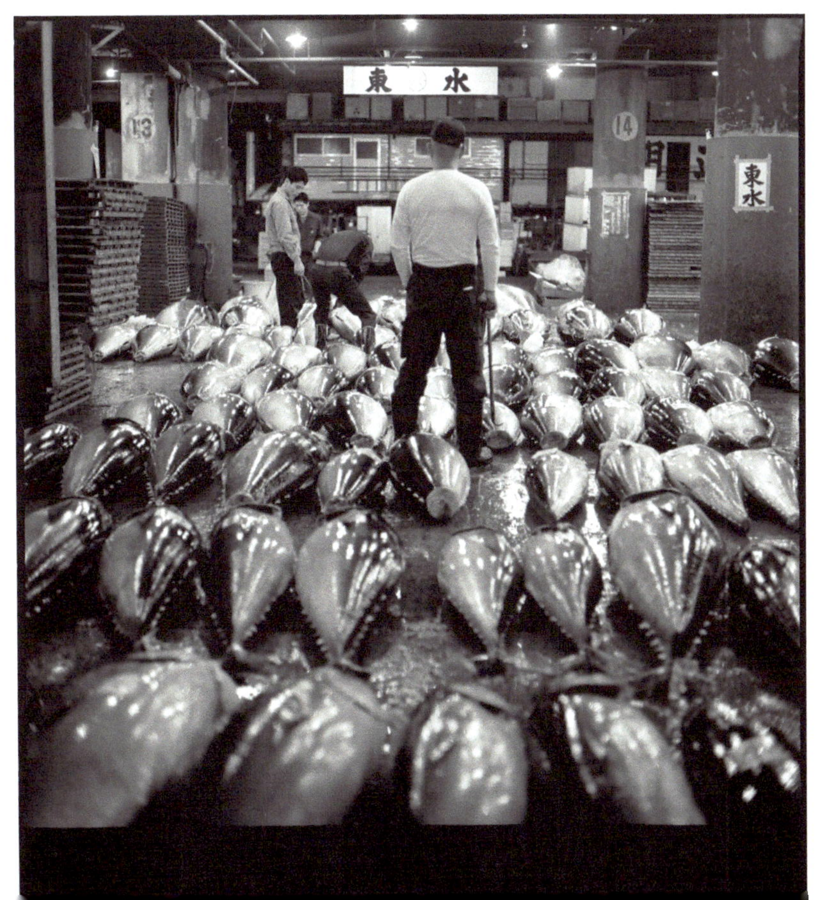

Introduction

Tsukiji, the place that gives the Tokyo Central Wholesale Market its common name, is somewhere between a well regulated machine and chaos. Stepping into the market is like stepping into a raging river where, if you don't quickly learn to navigate, you will drown under its activity. I stepped into this torrent for the first time in 1991, when nearly 3,000 tons of seafood was handled each day, making this the largest fish market in the world. The Tokyo Metropolitan Government plans to relocate the market because of its aging infrastructure. This small book is my homage to this place.

PRELUDE: From early evening through the early morning, trucks and ships deliver their cargo. By 3 am, this mass of seafood is being prepared for the morning auctions. The animal Tsukiji is most identified with is tuna. These giant fish, both fresh and frozen, are laid out in huge schools on the concrete floors. The climax comes at 5:30 am with the auctions.

COURANTE: The wholesale market comes to life. Fish from the auctions are distributed through the area on handcarts (pages 19, 37) or motorized vehicles known as *turrets* (page 36). Frozen tuna are cut up with band saws; fresh tuna are sectioned with sword-length knives. The transactions pass invisibly through long and deep connections between sellers and buyers—prices are rarely seen, except occasionally at the end of the day for last minute sales. By 11 am, the activity recedes like the tide.

INTERMEZZO: In early afternoon, Tsukiji is deserted. A soft natural light penetrates the 1935 market building. Tsukiji is strangely peaceful; only a muted, distant drone reminds you that you are in the economic center of one of the world's largest cities. But this peace is only a temporary interlude before the cycle begins again.

築地は、東京都中央卸売市場としても知られているが、中の様子はまるでうまく制御された機械と大混乱の間と言えばいいのか。足を踏み入れれば、荒れ狂う川に飛び込んだも同じで、すぐに流れに乗っていくことを覚えなければ、市場の動きにのまれて溺れてしまう。私が築地のこの激流に飛び込んだのは1991年で、世界最大の市場として、当時は毎日およそ3000トンの海産物が取引されていた。東京都は今、施設の老朽化にともない、市場の移転を検討している。この小さな本「築地－東京魚市場組曲」を、築地への敬意として捧げる。

プレリュード：夕方から早朝にかけて、トラックや船がカーゴを運んできて大量の海産物を下ろし、午前3時には競りに向けた準備が始まる。築地は、マグロで有名だ。新鮮なものや冷凍ものなど、マグロの大群がコンクリートの床に並べられる。午前5時30分には競りが始まり、築地はクライマックスに達する。

クーラント：卸売市場が目を覚ます。競り落とされた魚が、競り場からカート(pages 19, 37)やターレット(page 36)で運ばれていく。帯のこぎりで冷凍マグロが、鮪包丁で新鮮なマグロが解体されていく。売買は、素人の目には見えない。買い手と売り手が長い間に築いた深い関係を通して行われるので、値札を見るのは稀で、市場が閉まる寸前のセール時ぐらいだけだ。こうした取引も、11時までには潮が引くように終る。

間奏曲：昼過ぎ、築地に人の姿はない。柔らかな自然光が、1935年に造られた市場に差し込む。奇妙な静けさだ。市場の外から聞こえてくる弱く低い音だけが、世界でもっとも大きな都市のひとつの経済の中心地にいることを思い出させる。

Prelude

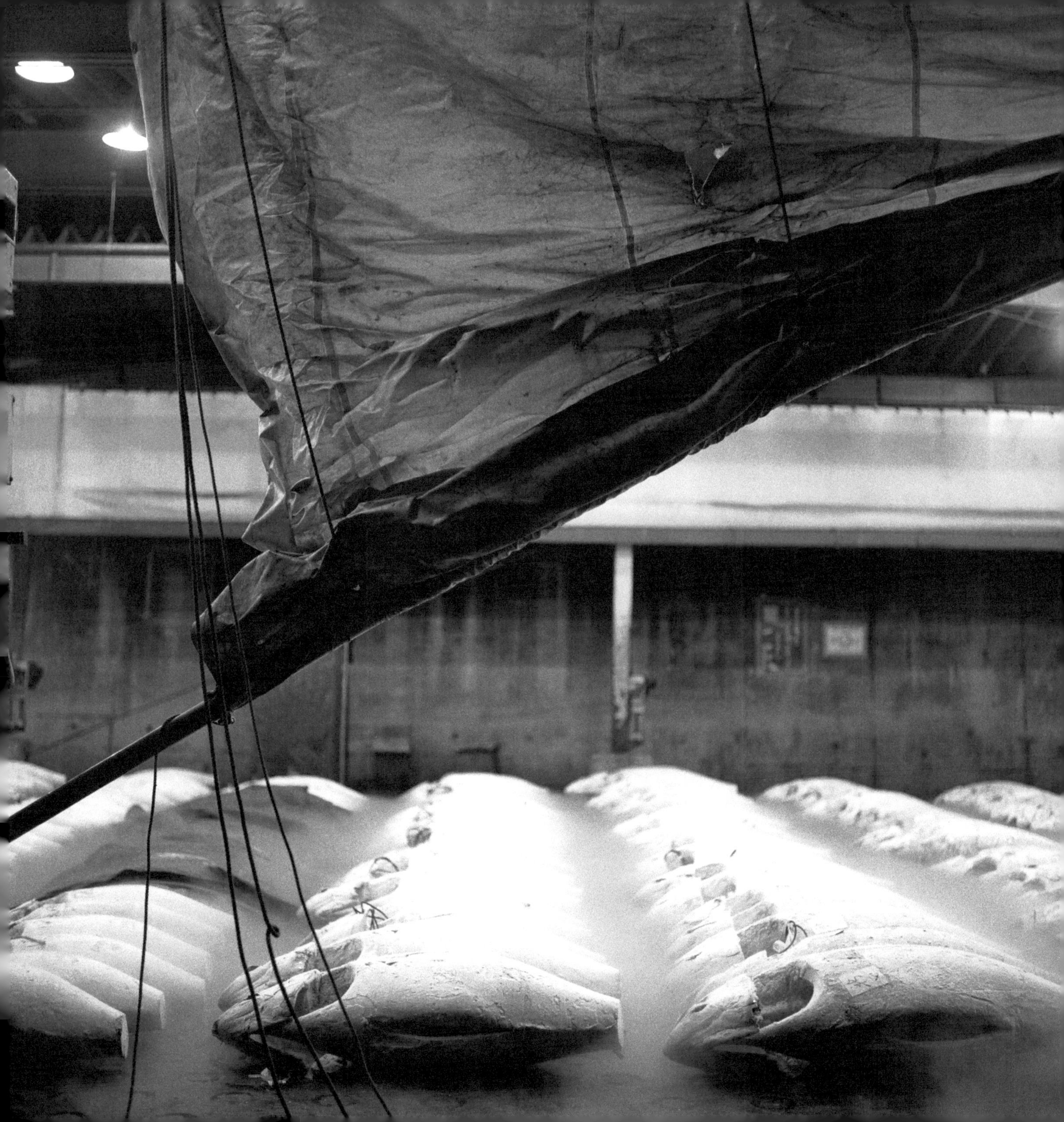

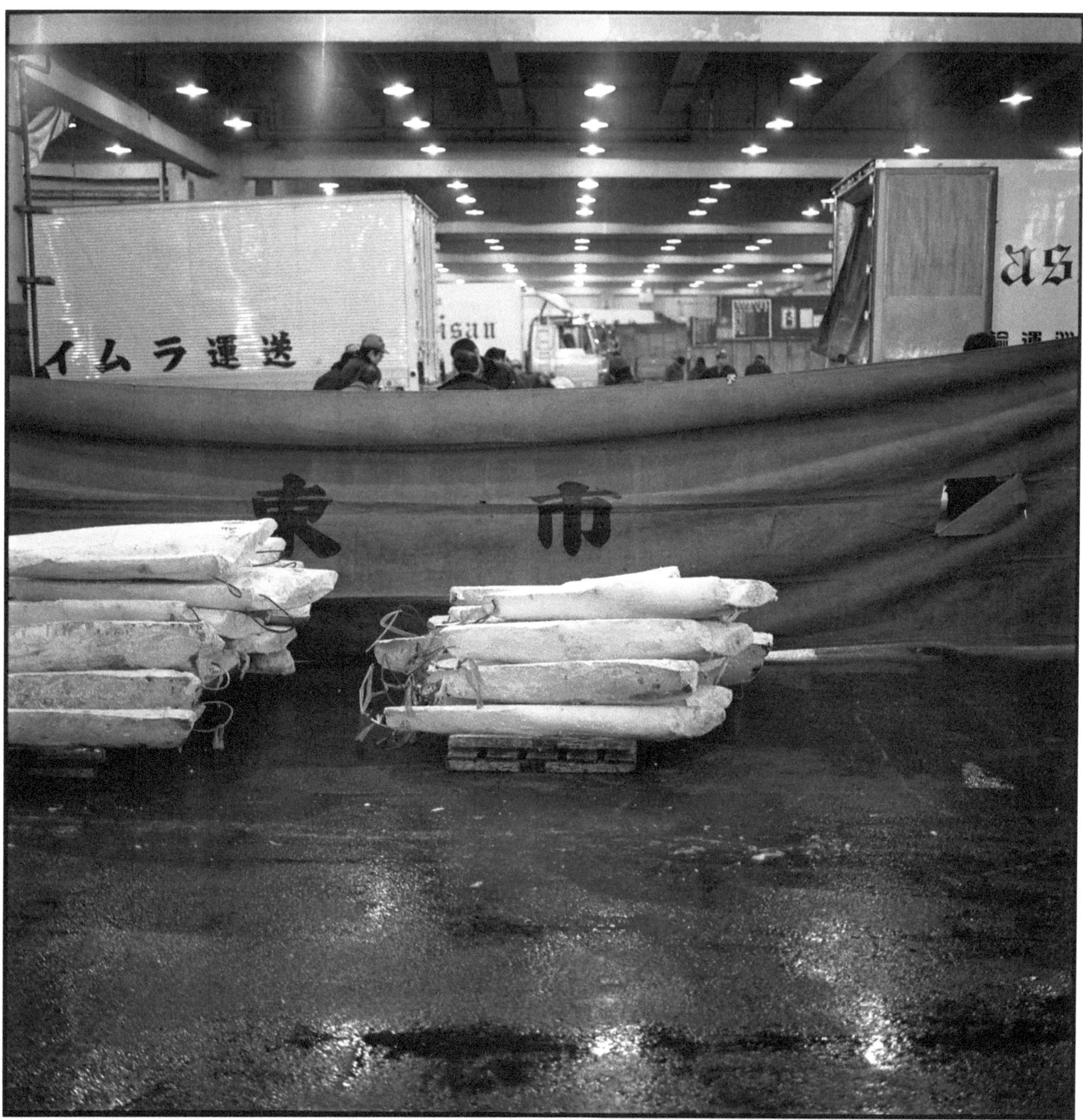
イムラ運送
東　市

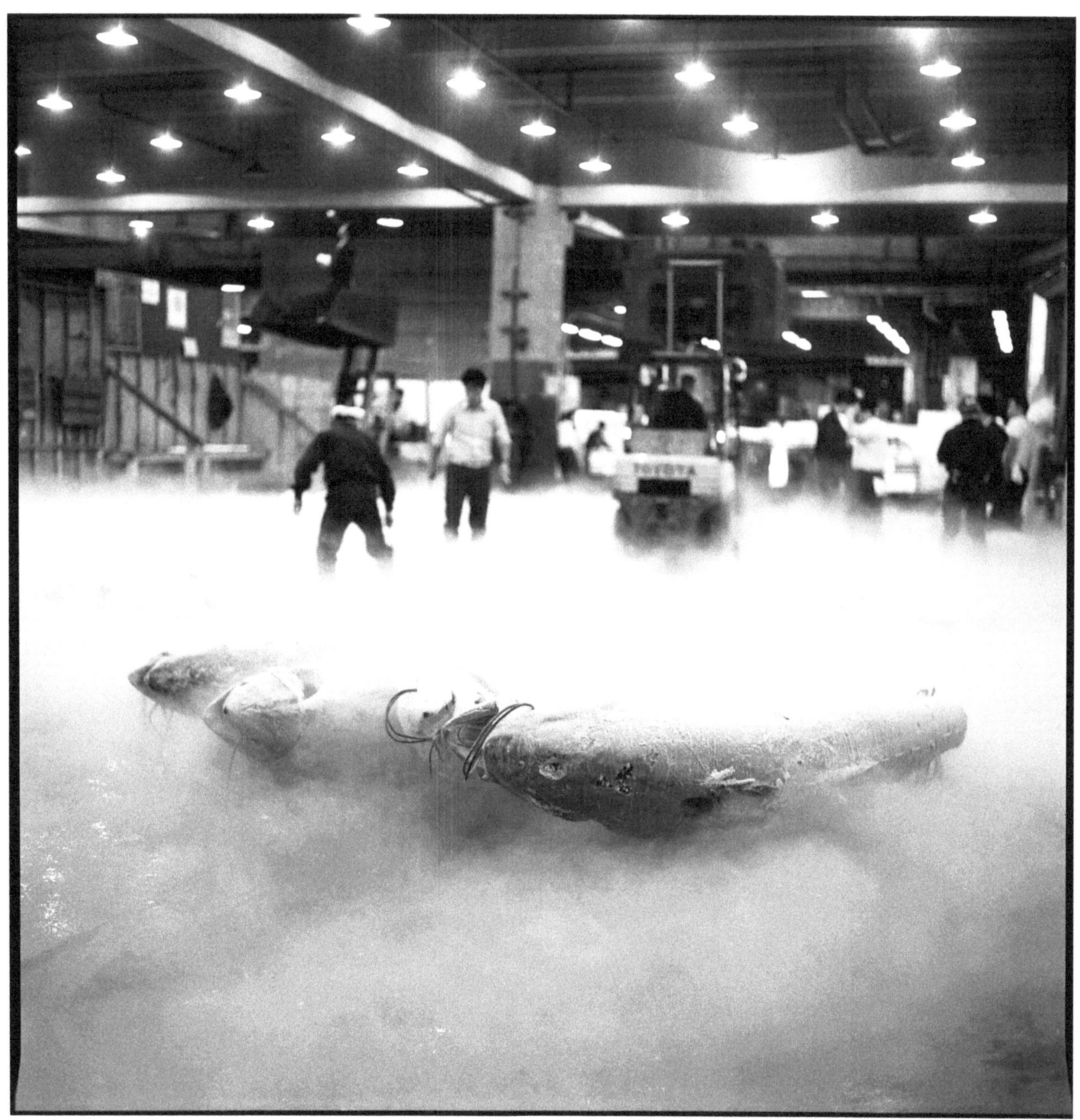

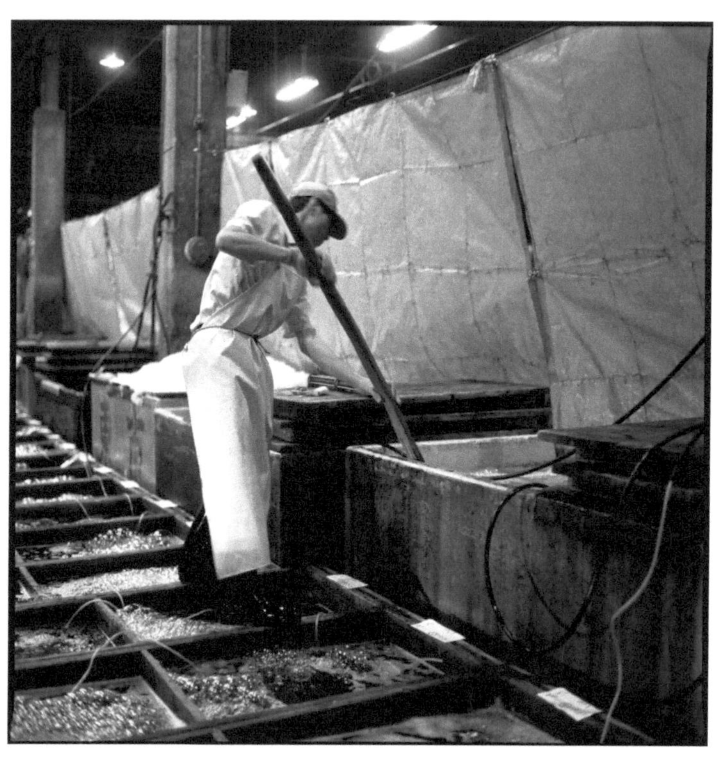

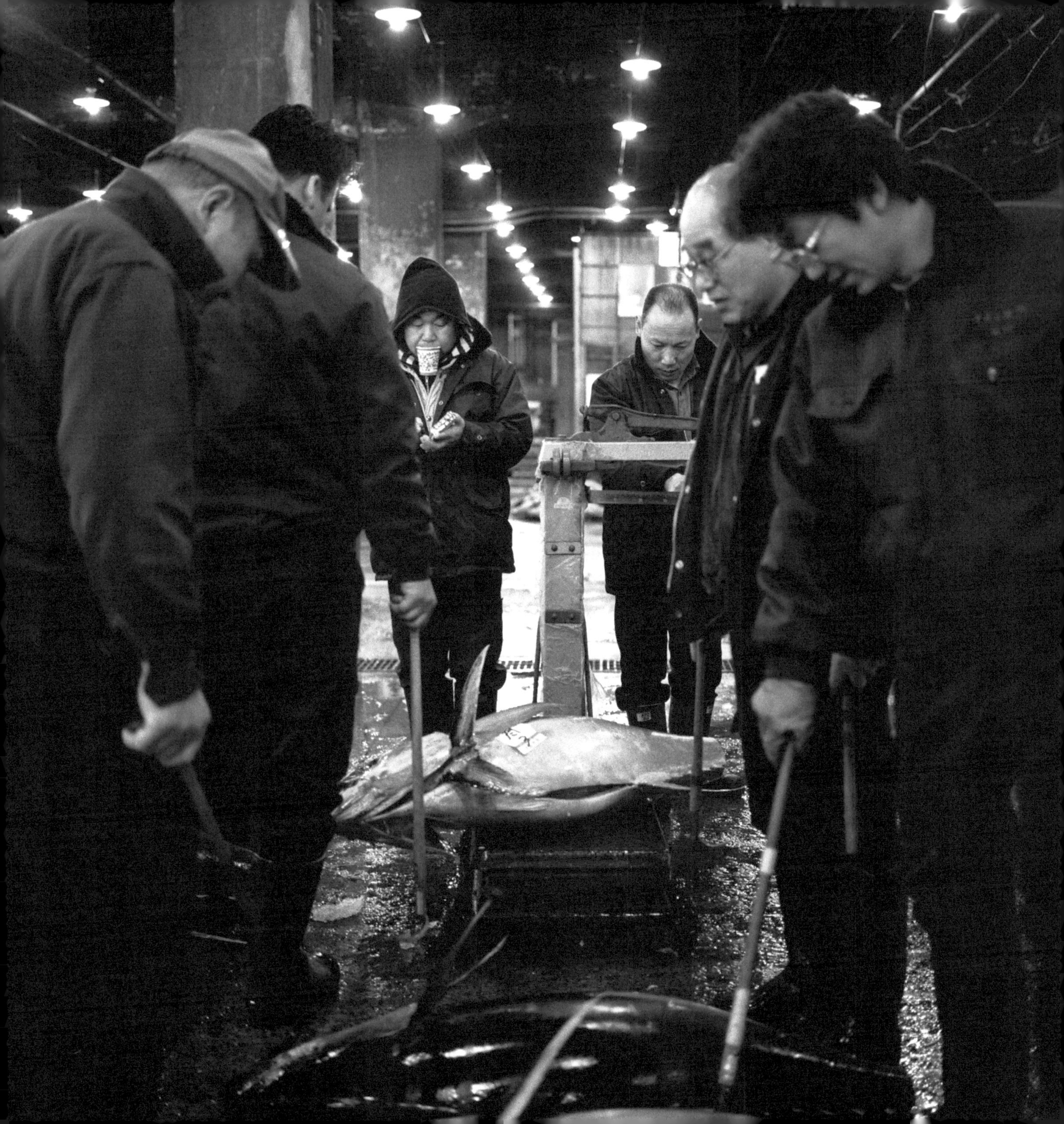

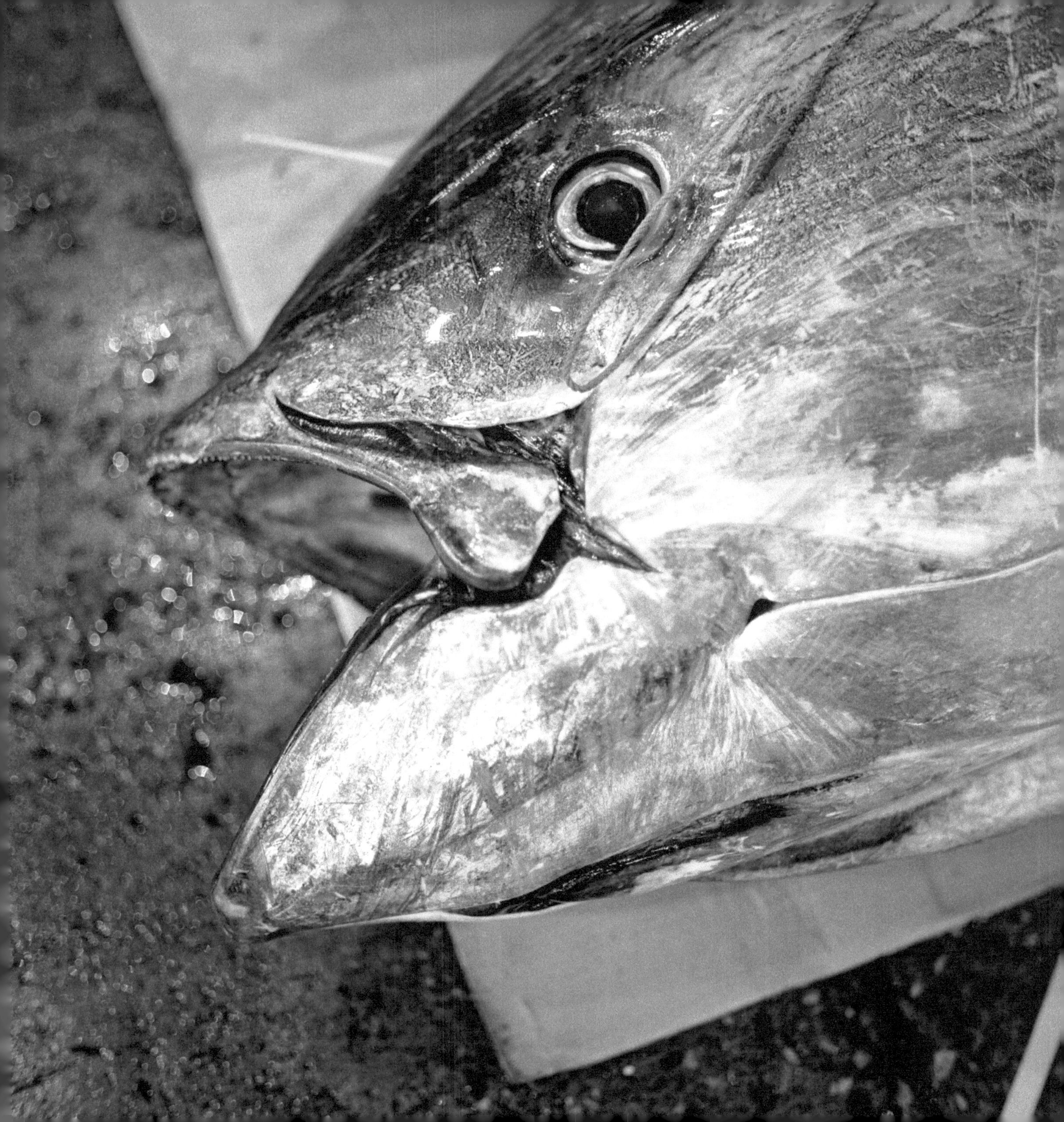

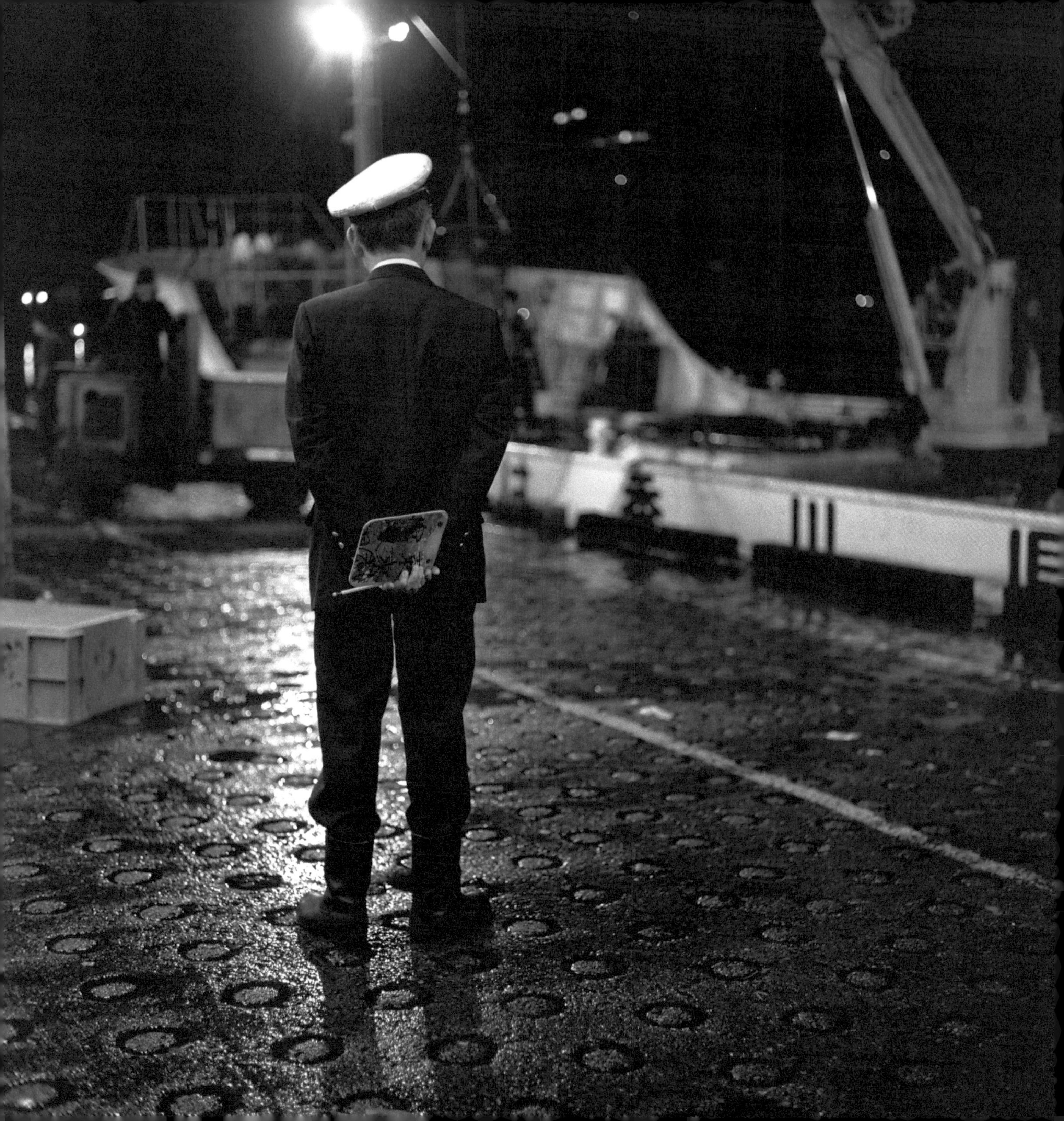

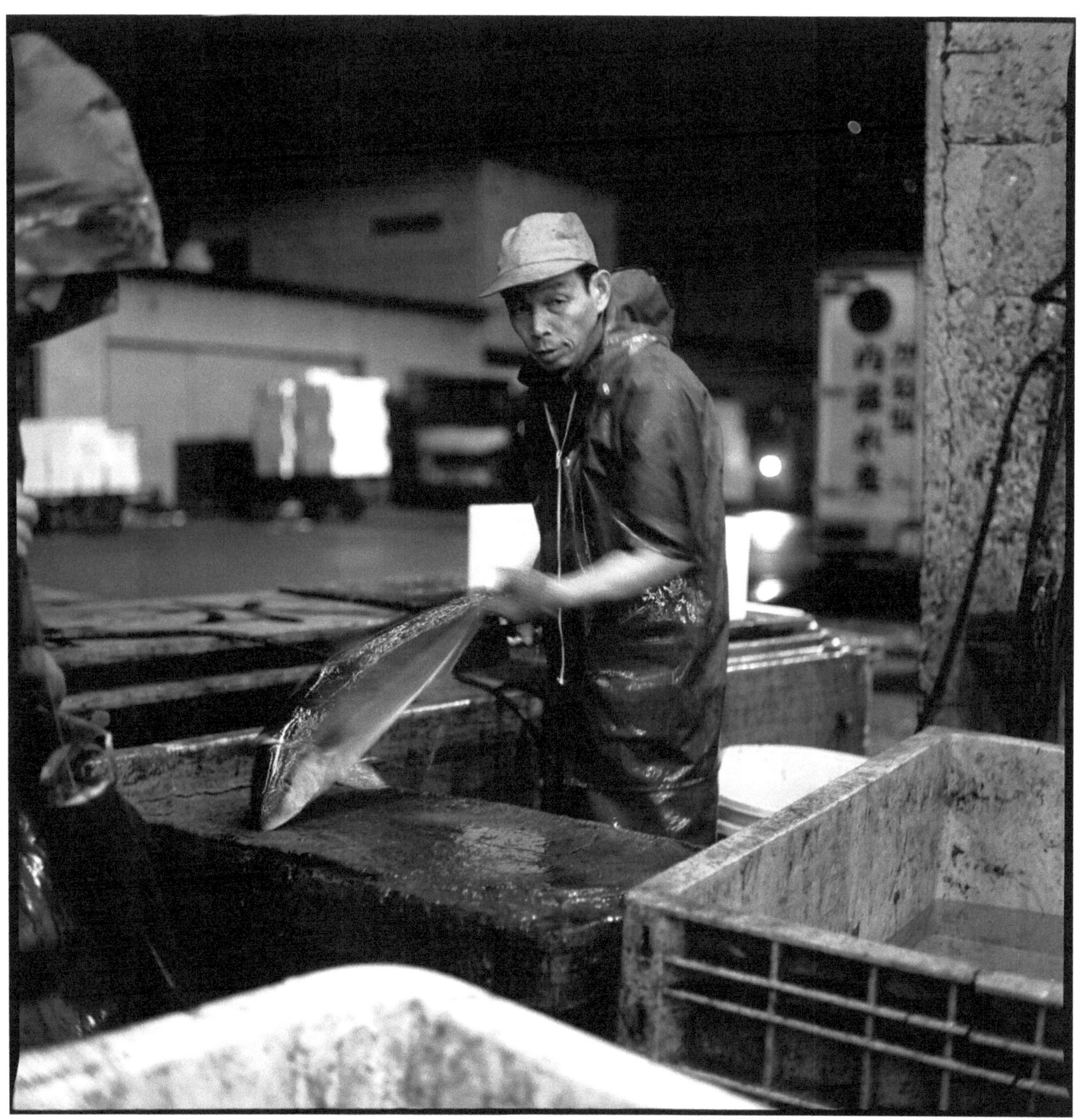

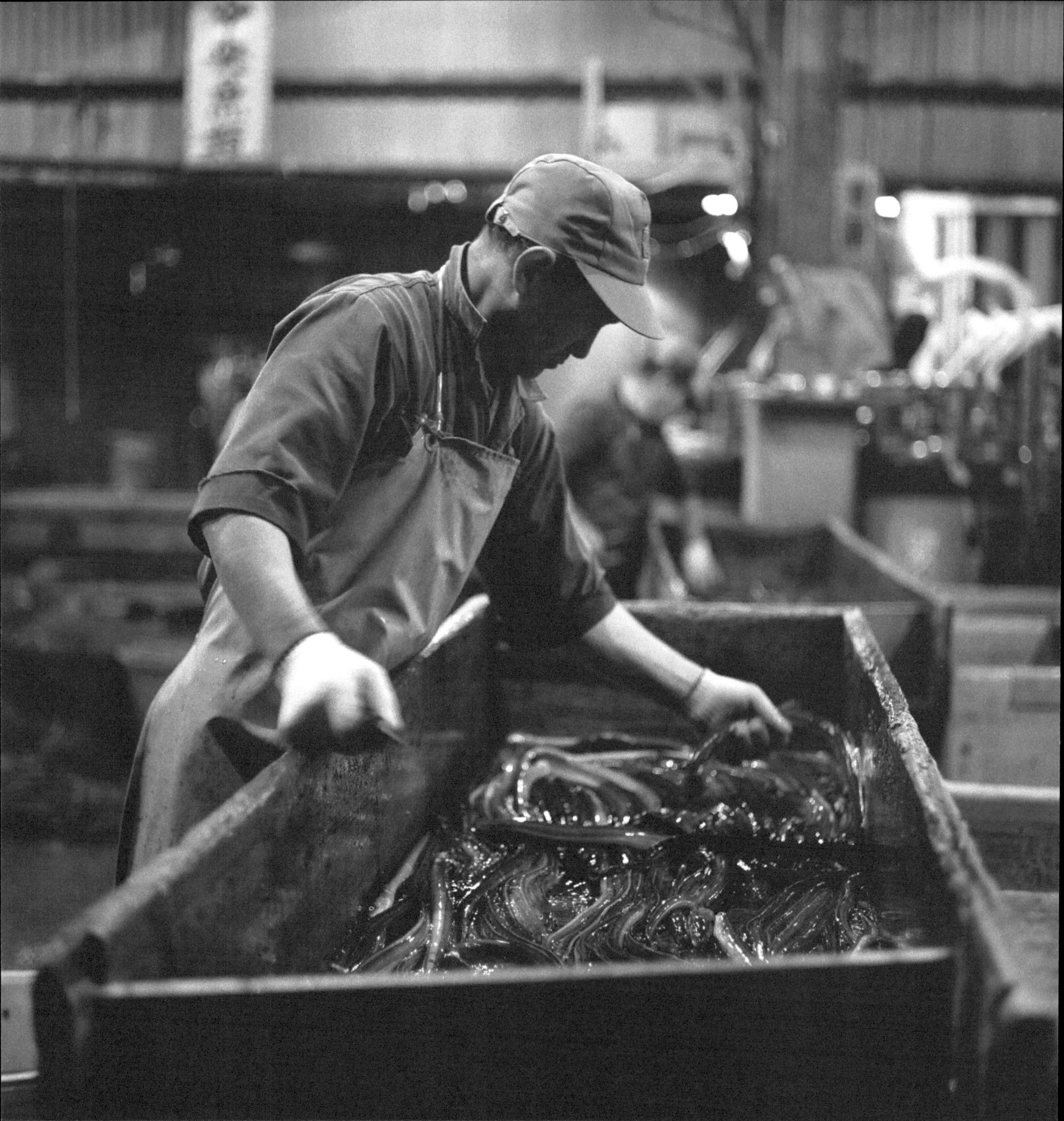

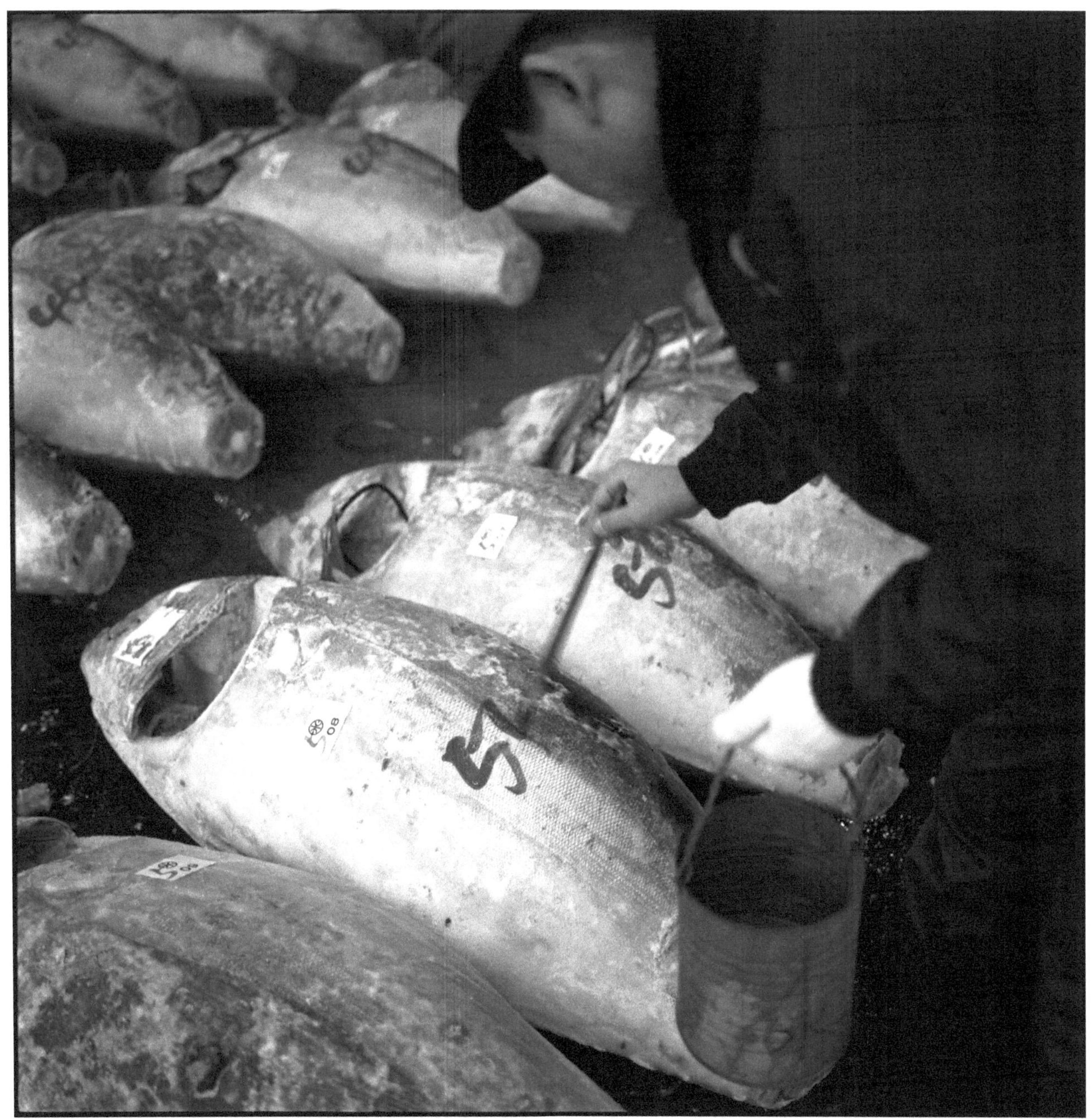

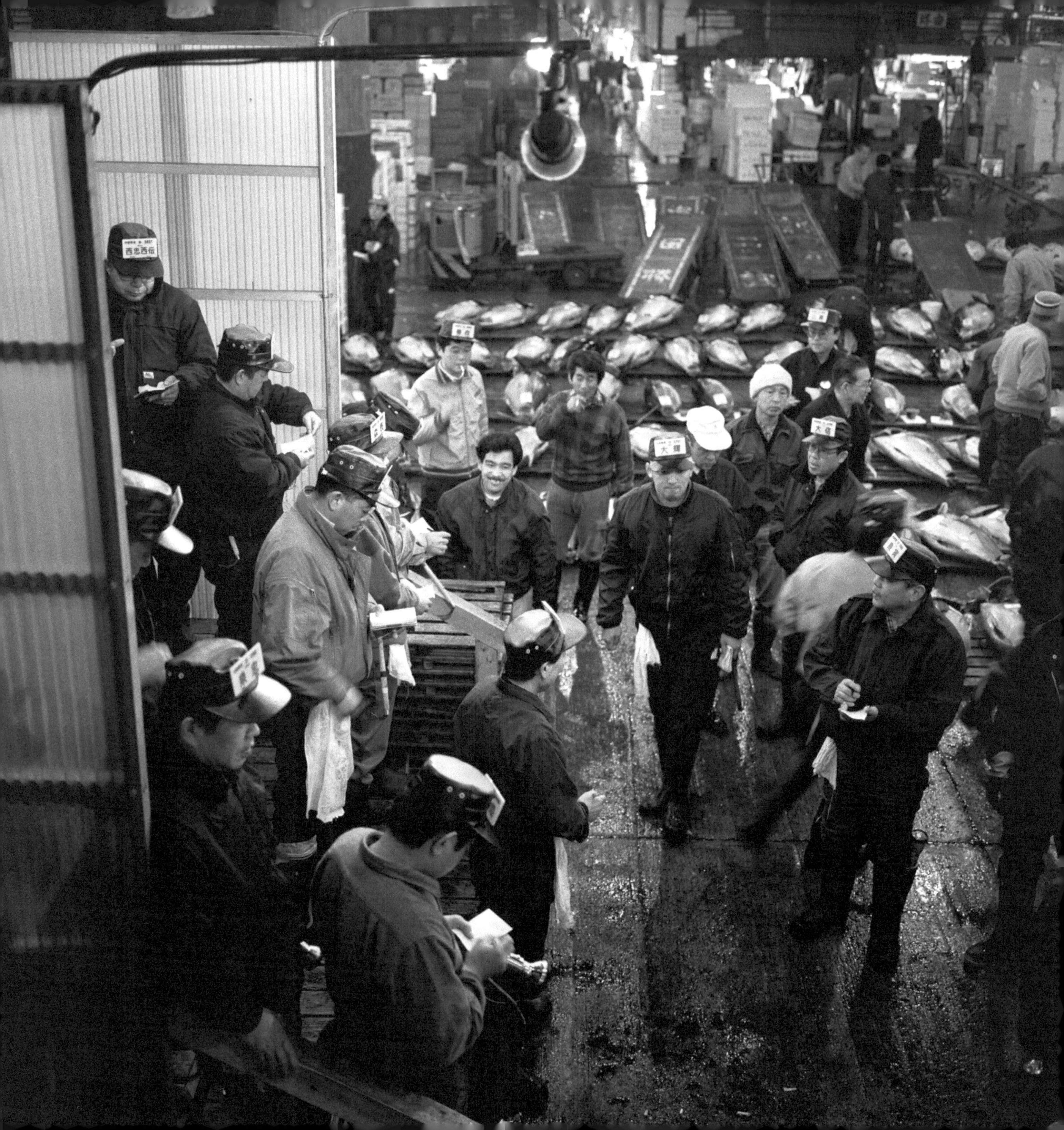

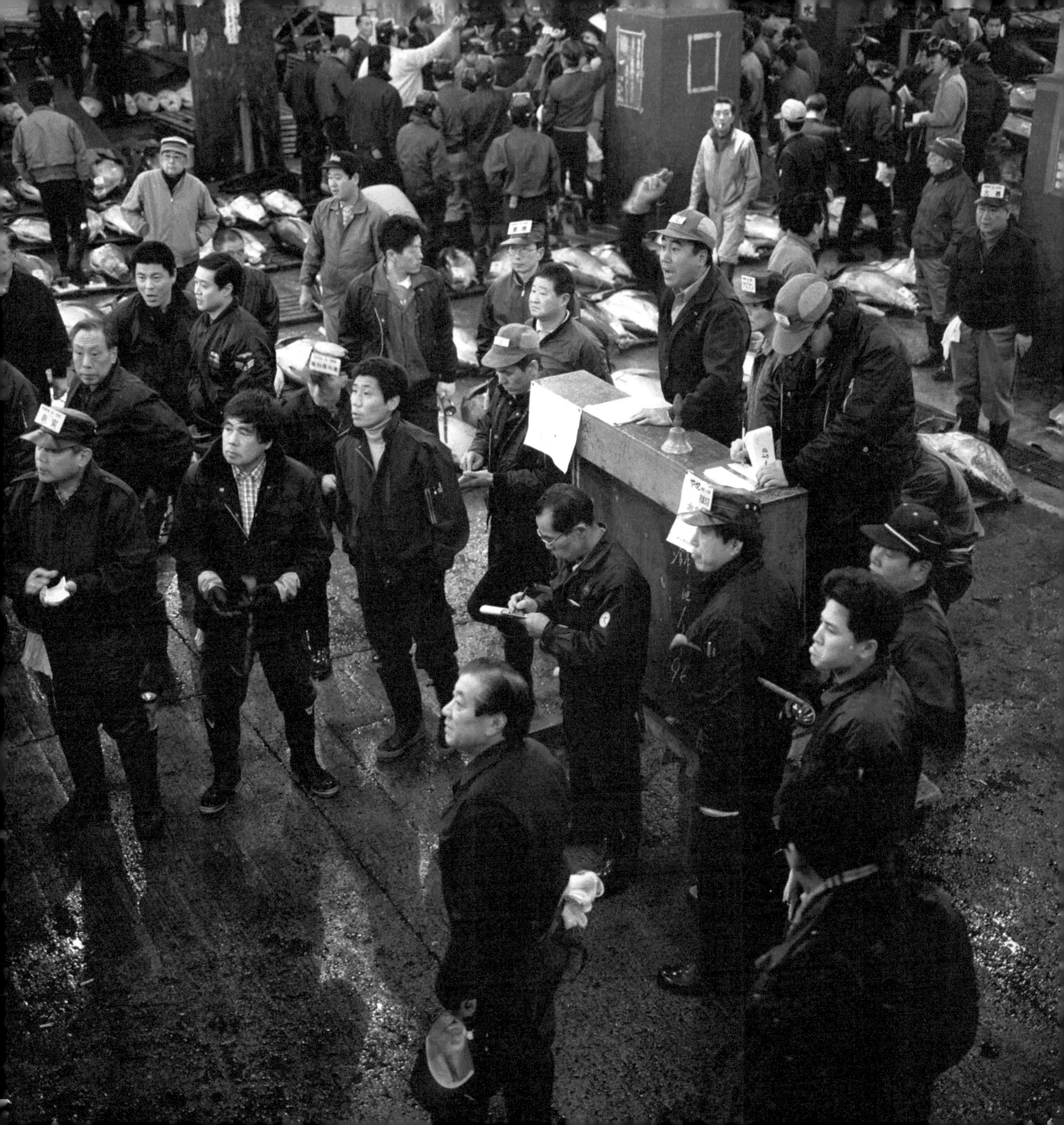

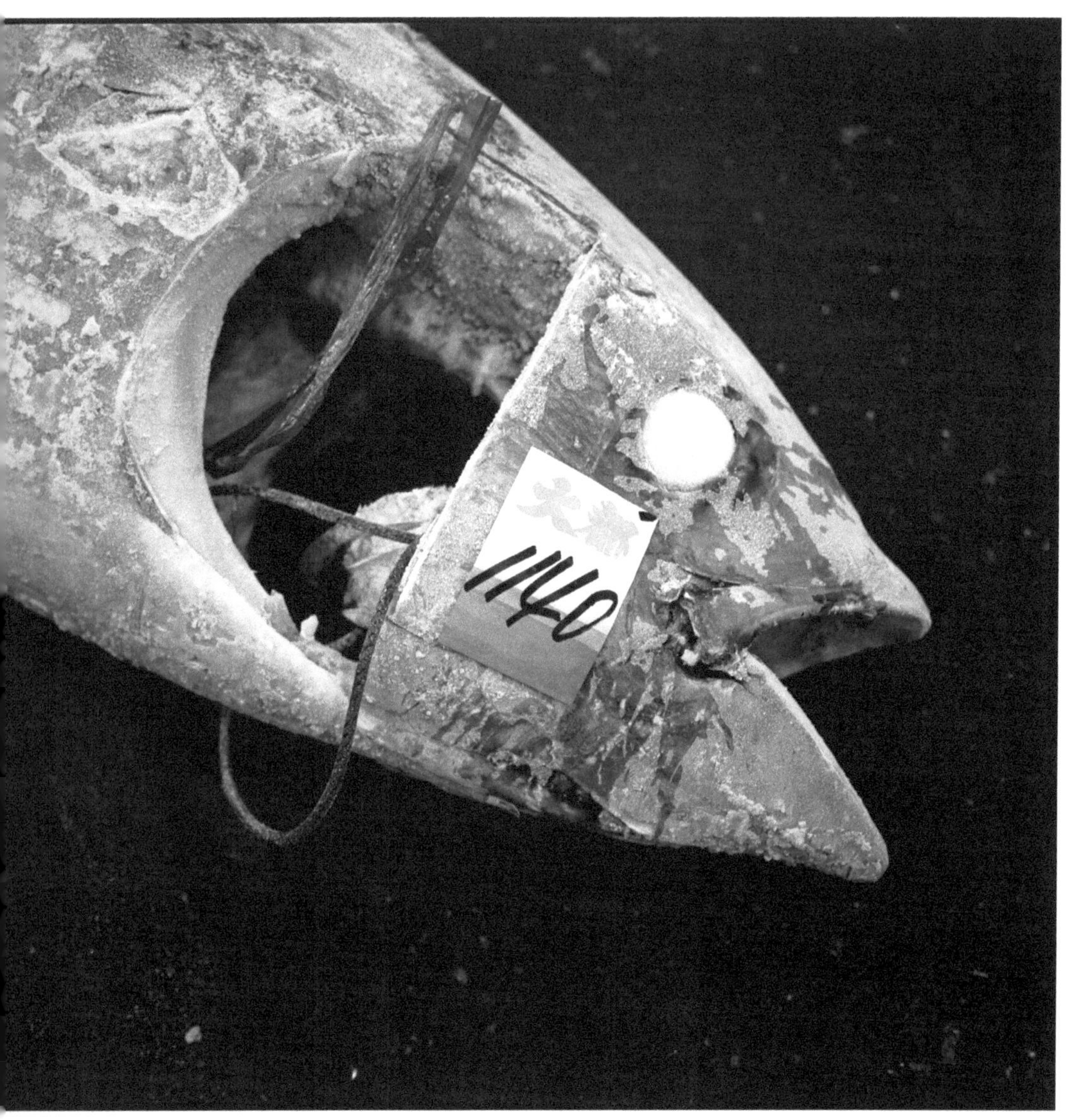
11140

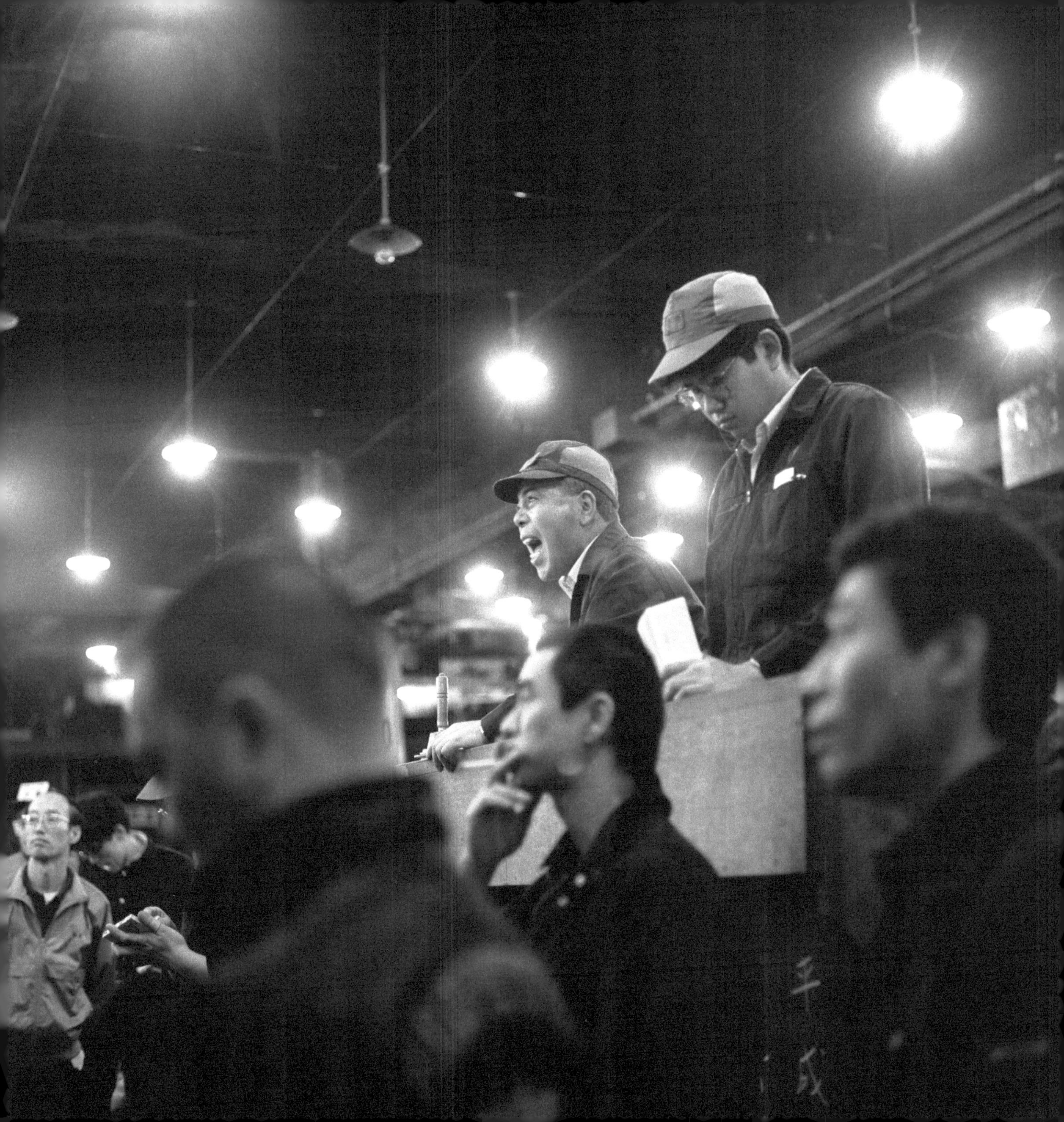

Courante

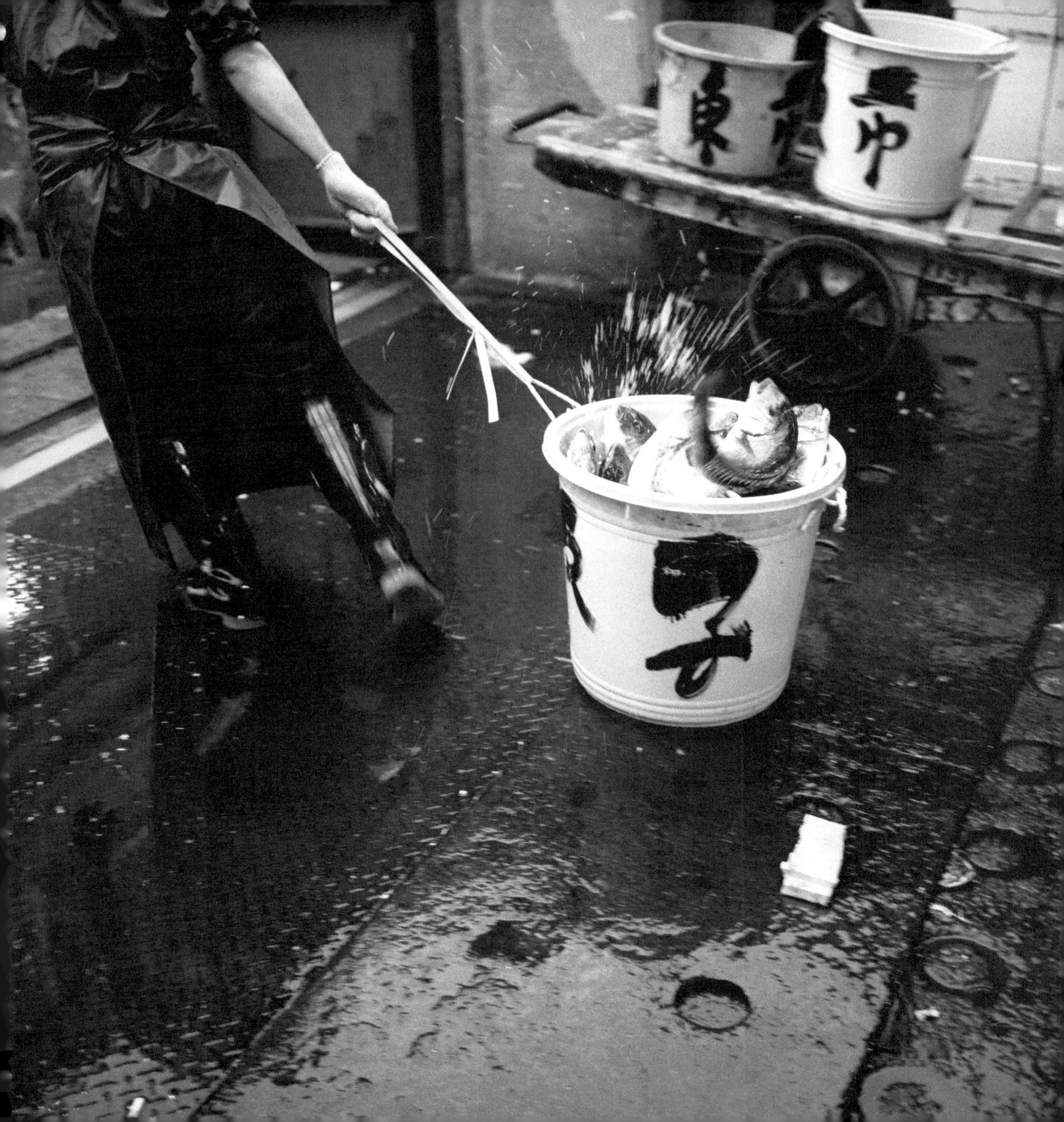

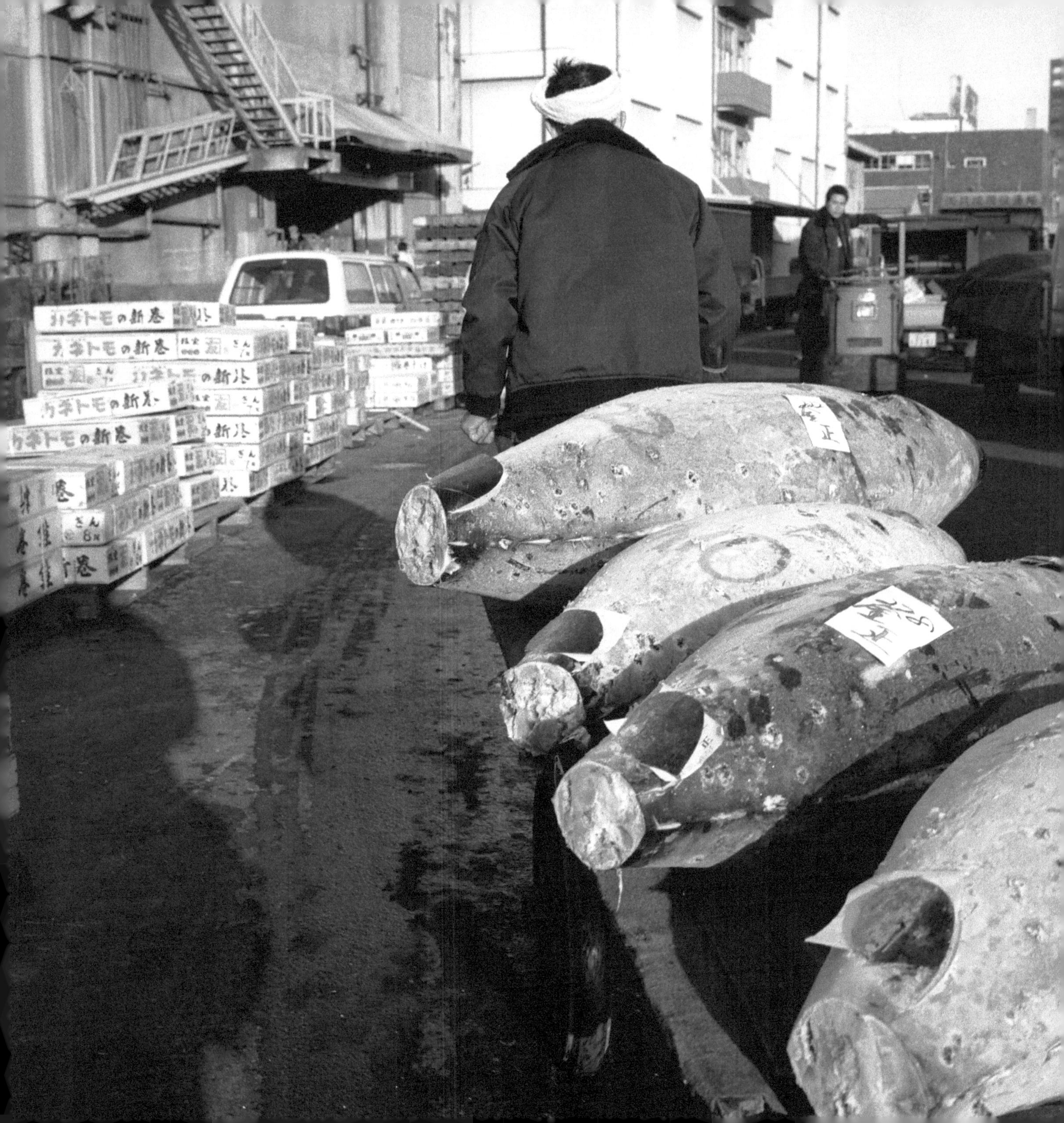

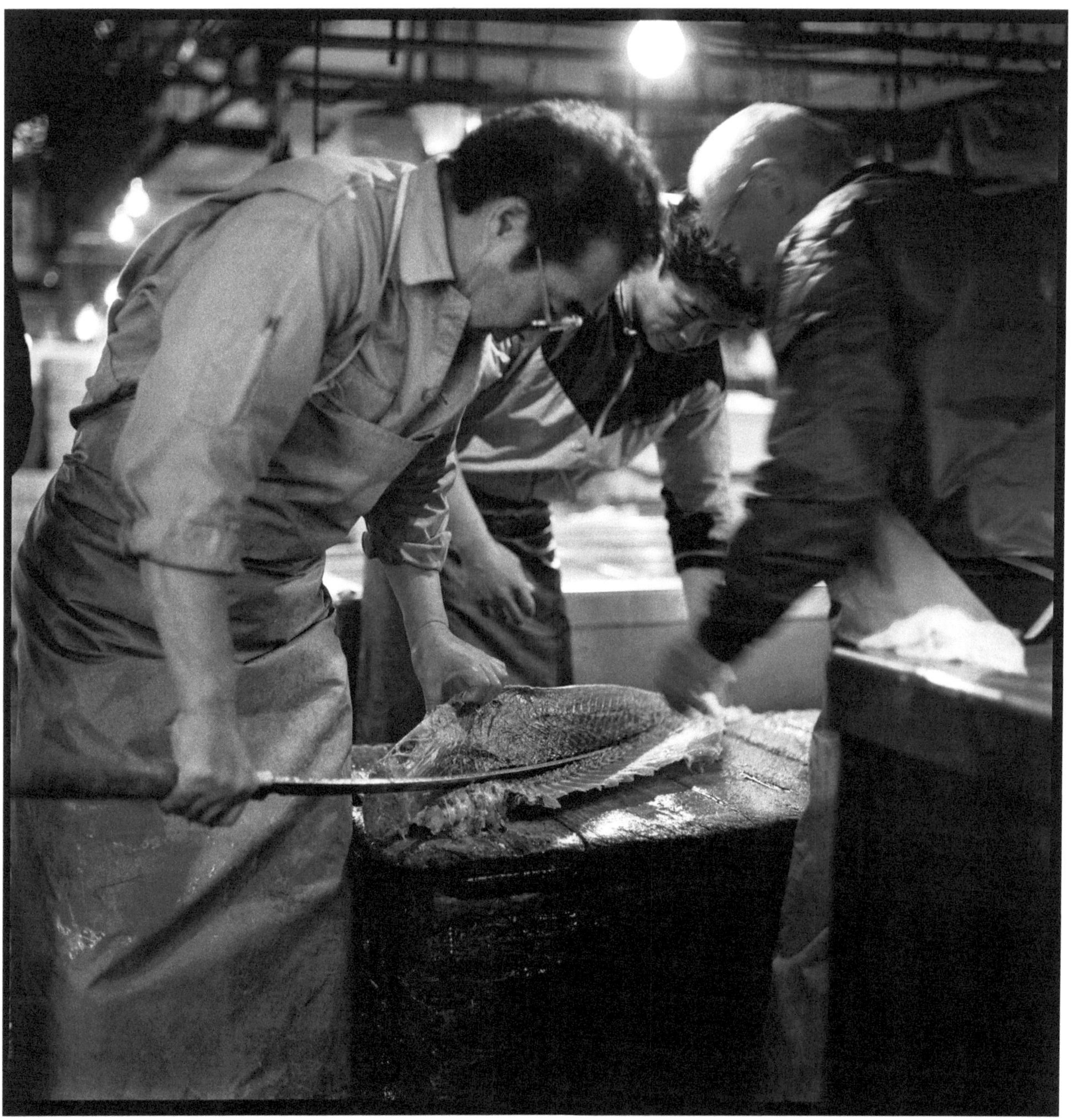

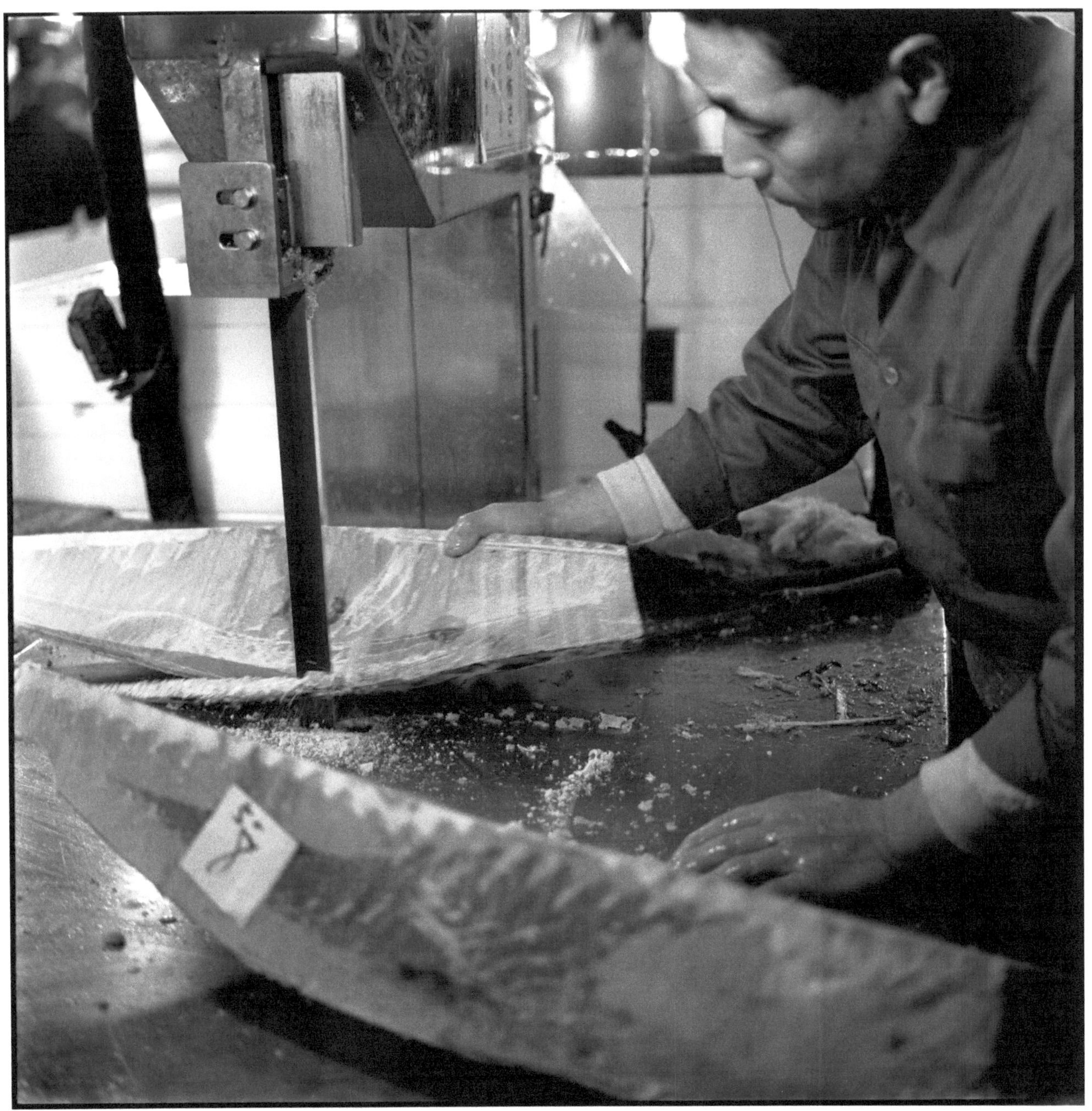

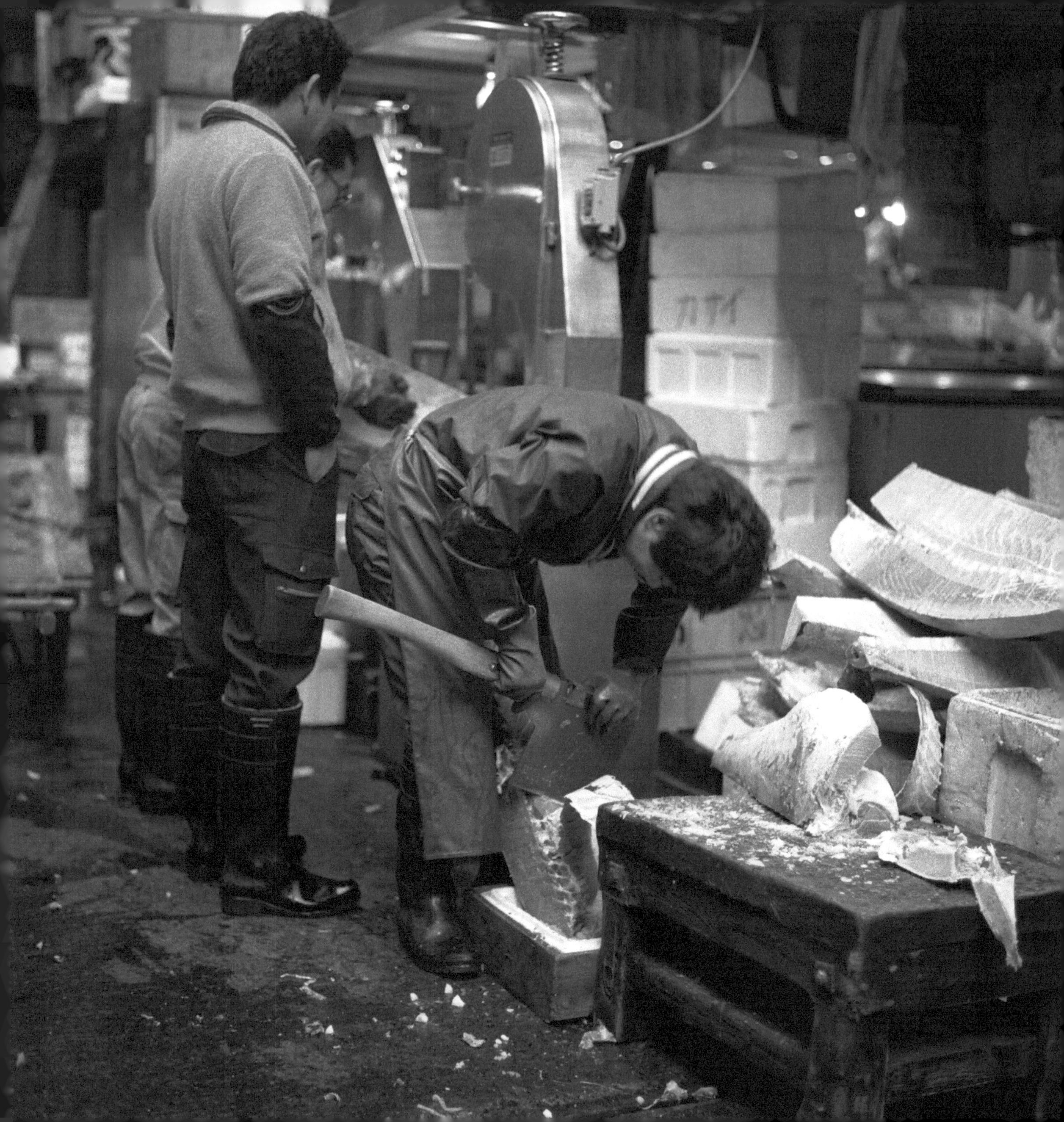

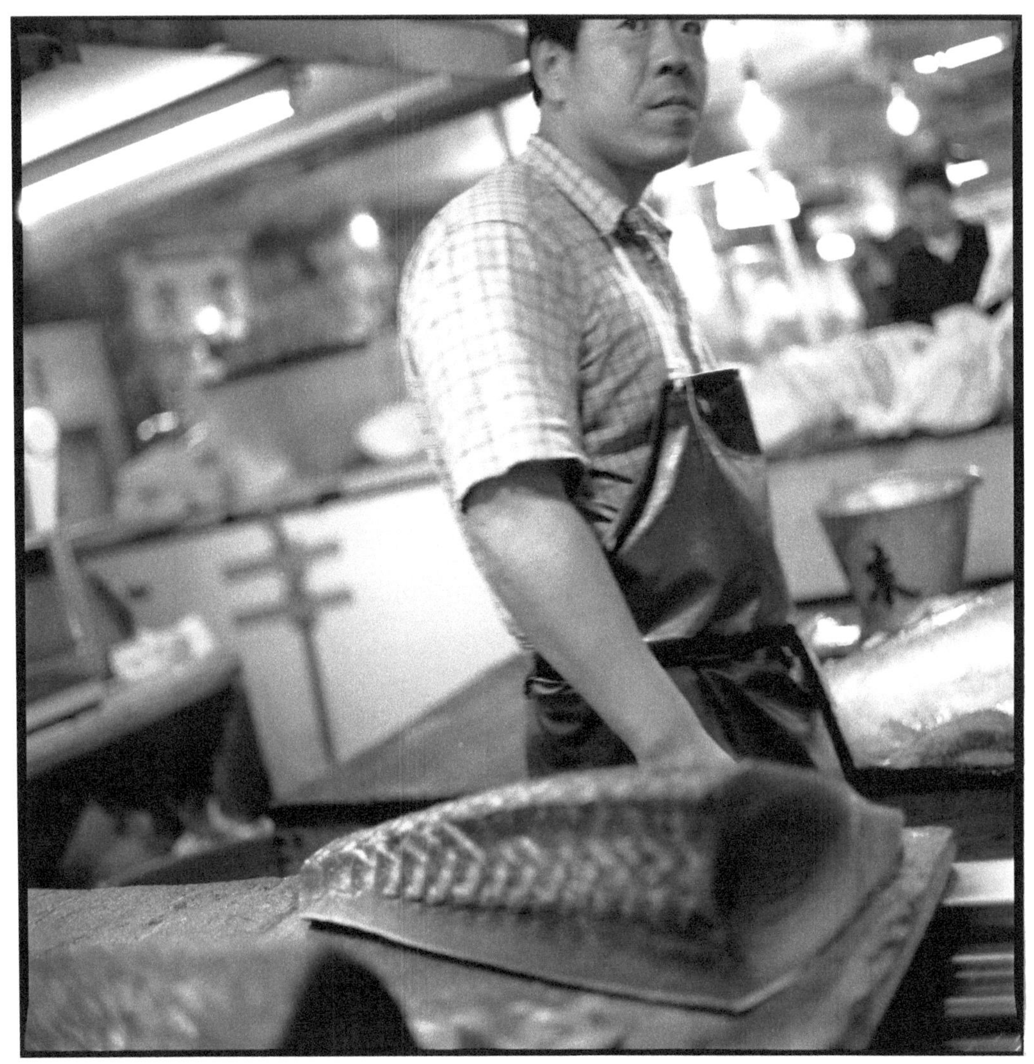

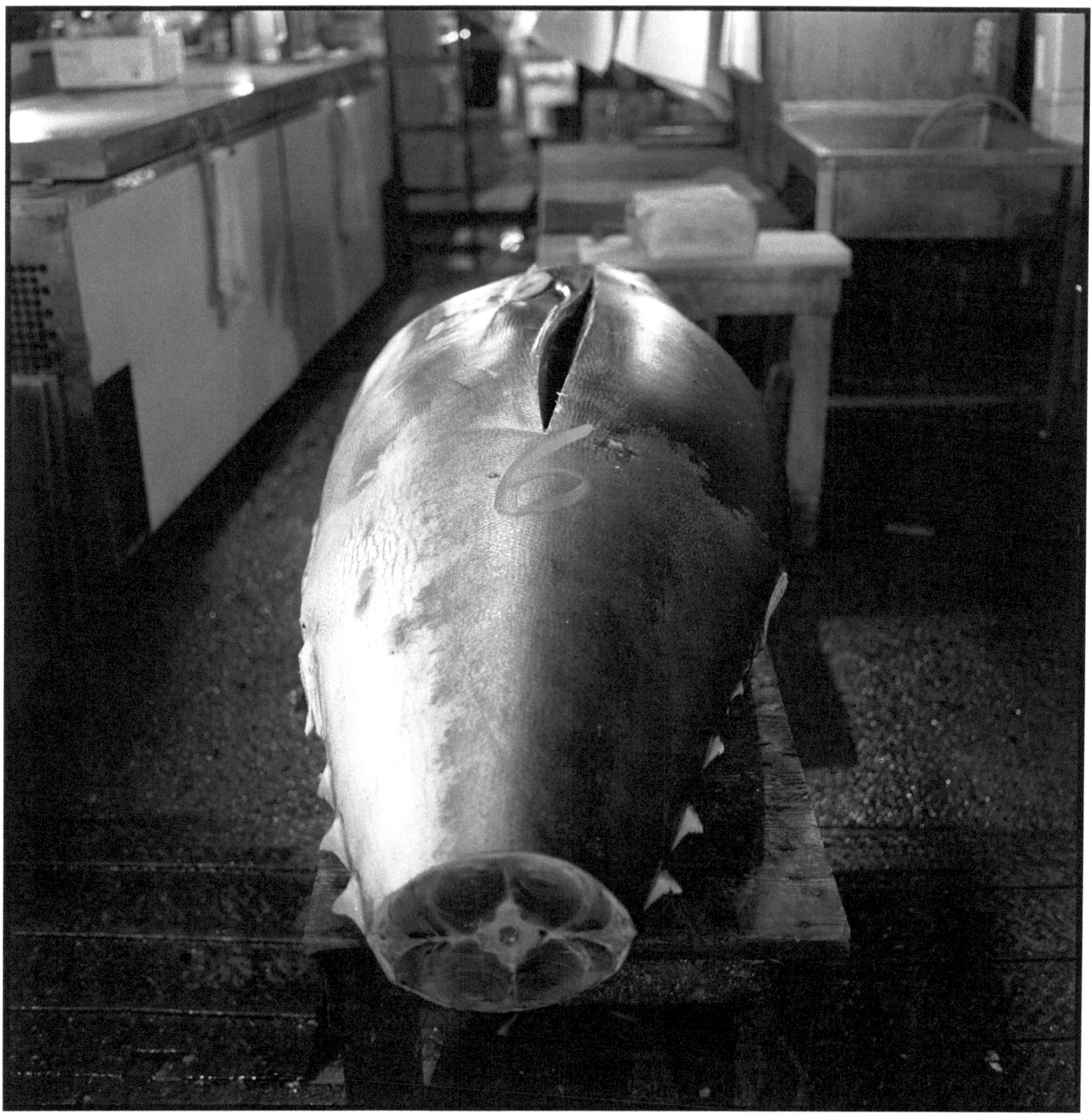

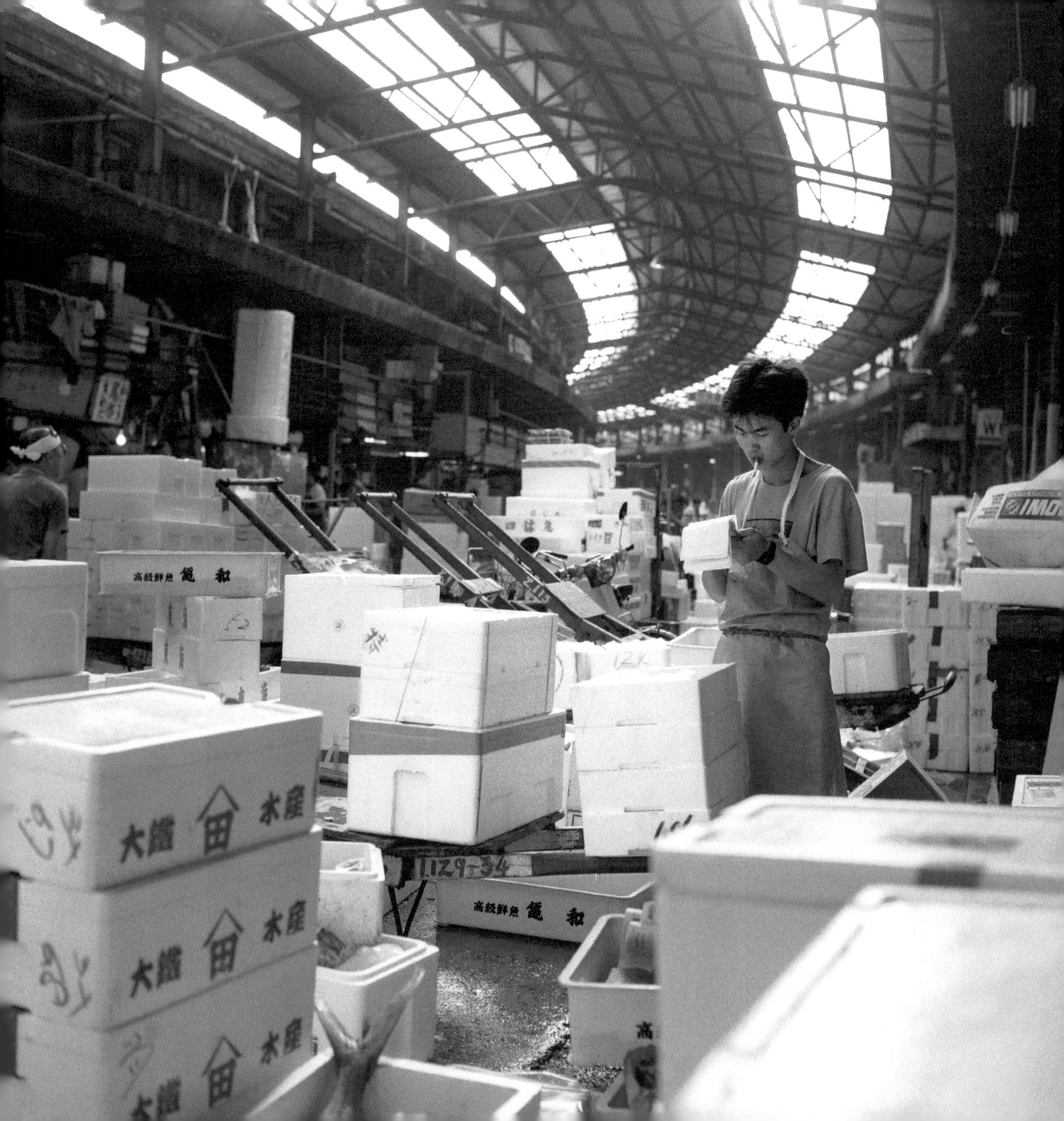

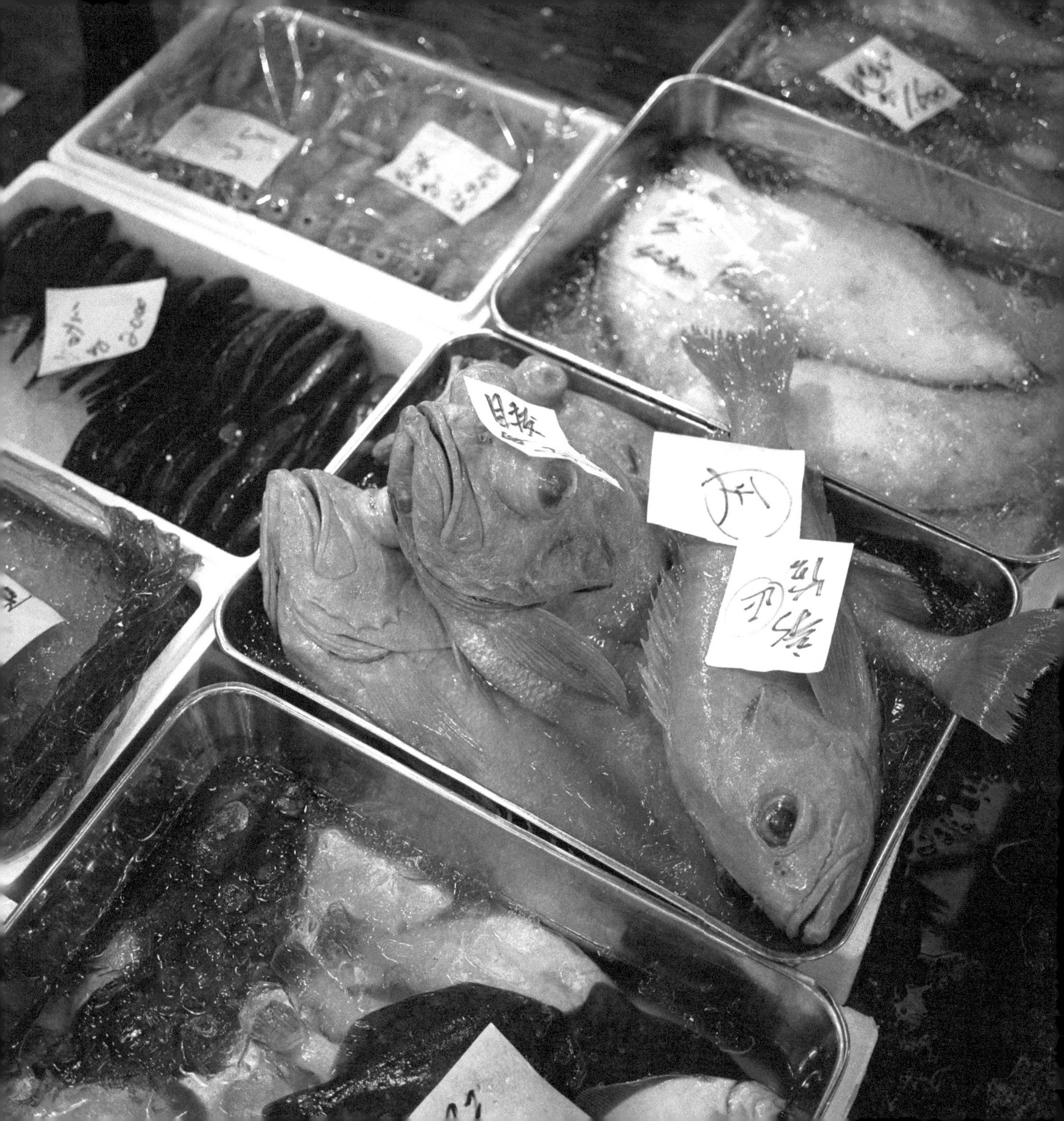

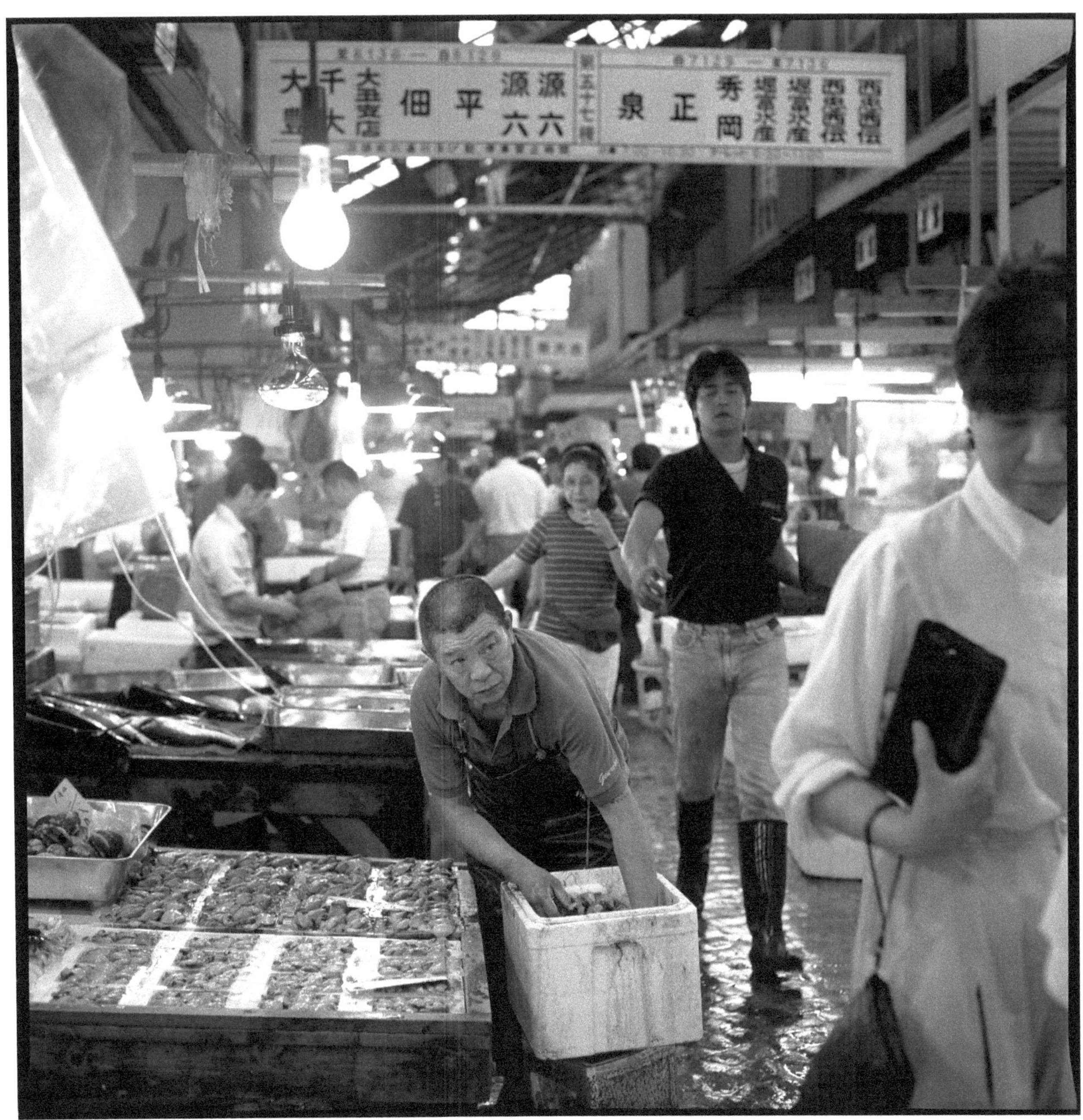
大千大佃平源源第泉正秀堀堀西西
豊大店六六五岡富富水水
十水水産信
七産産
番

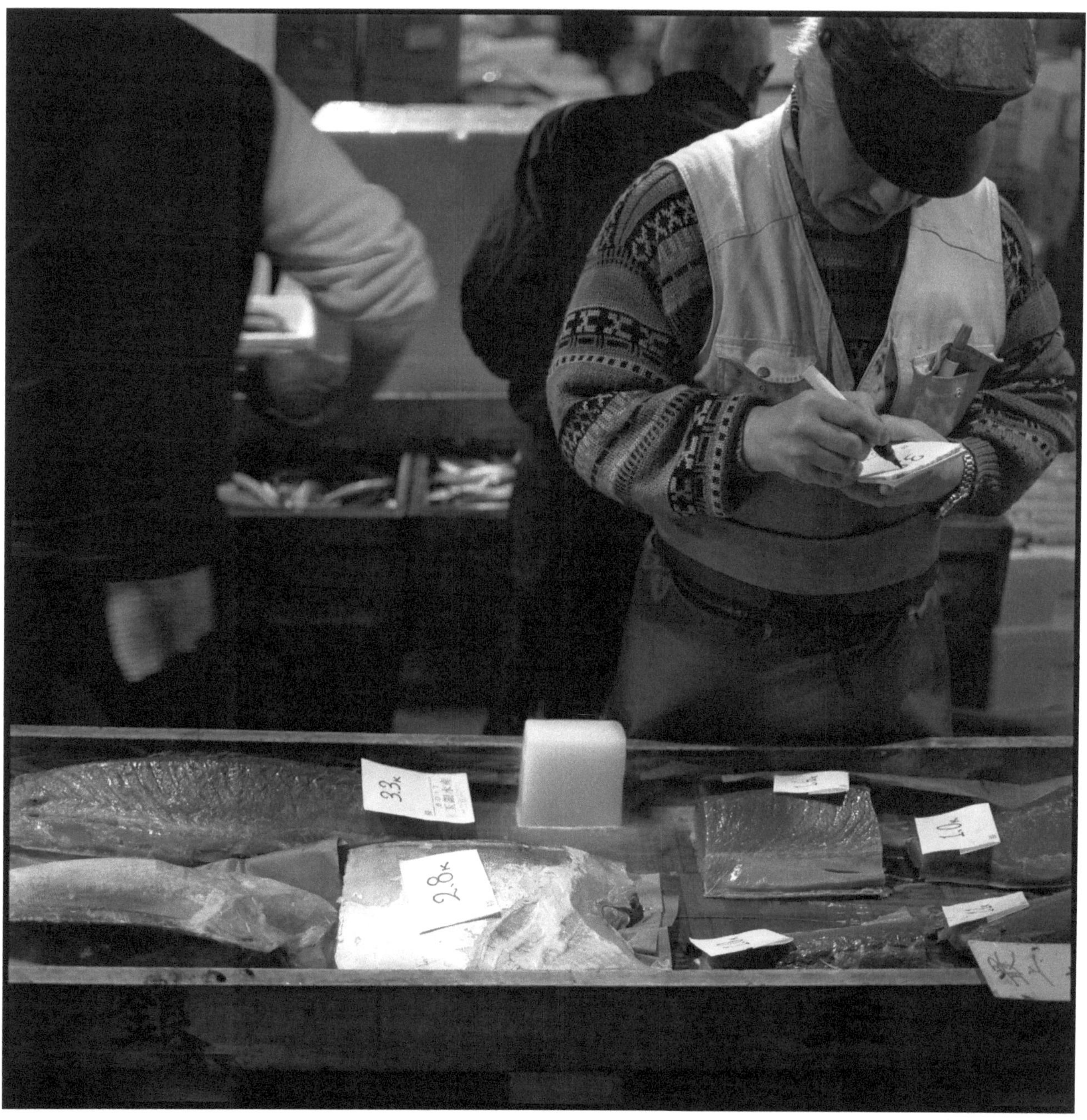

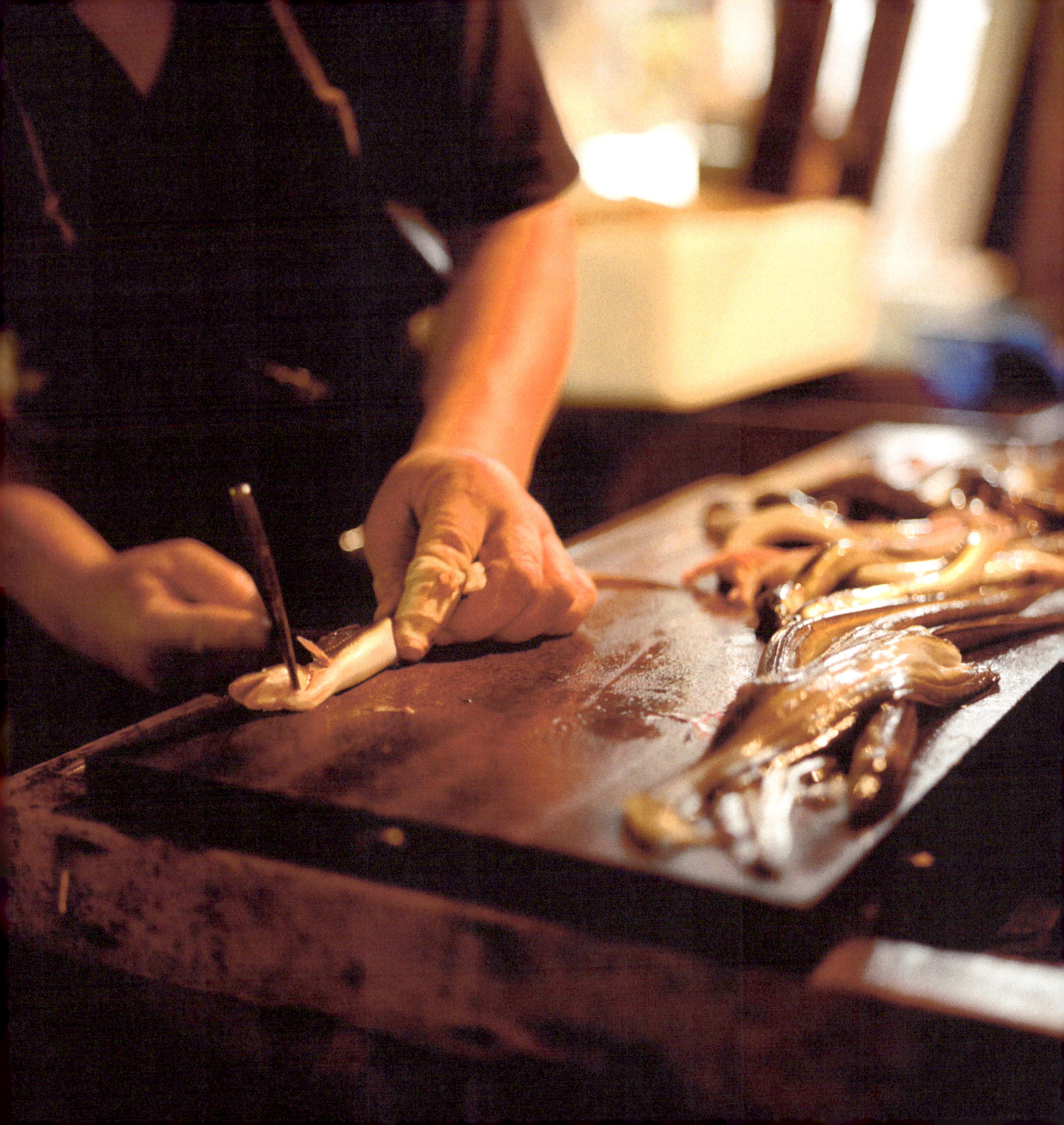

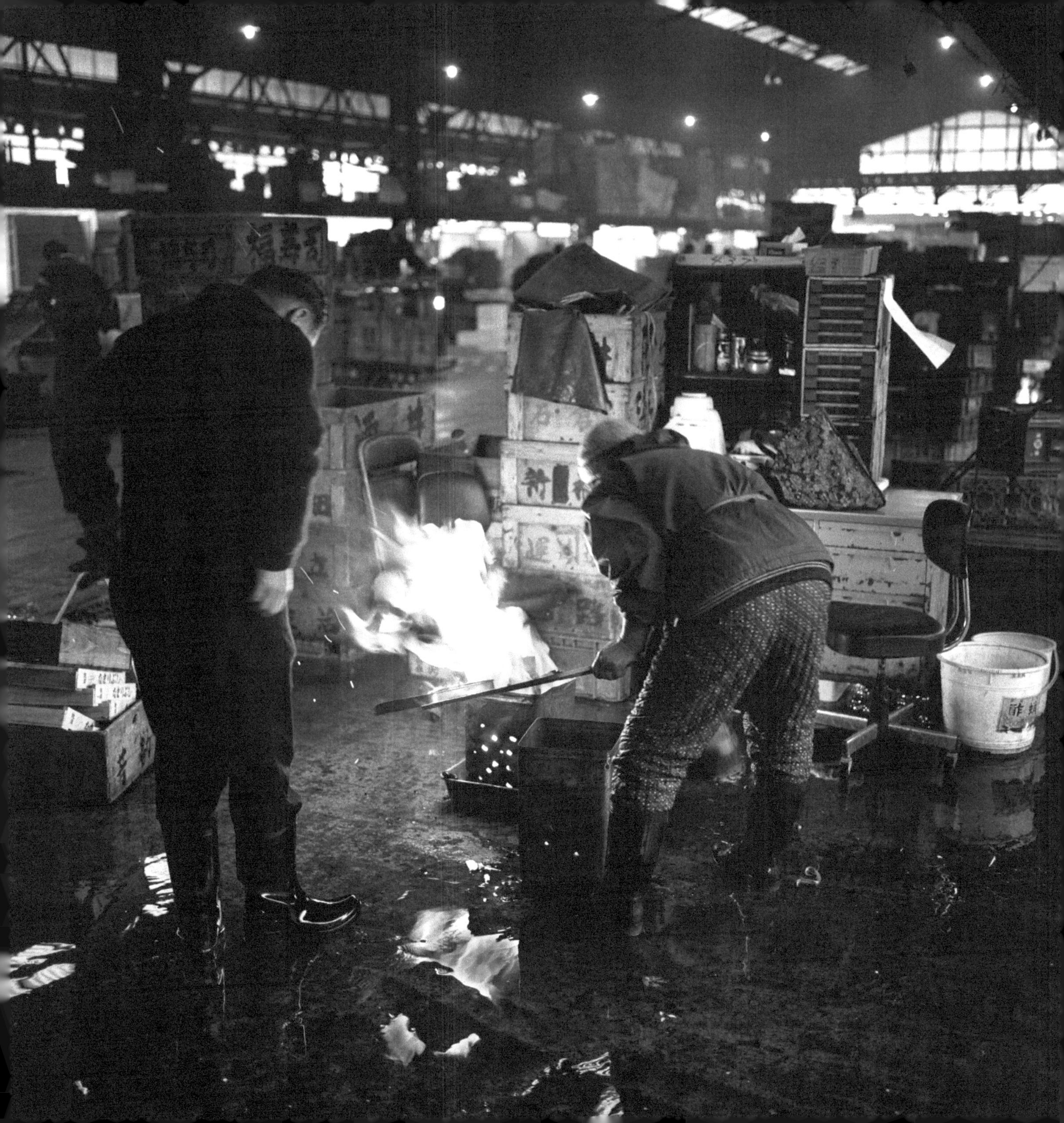

Intermezzo

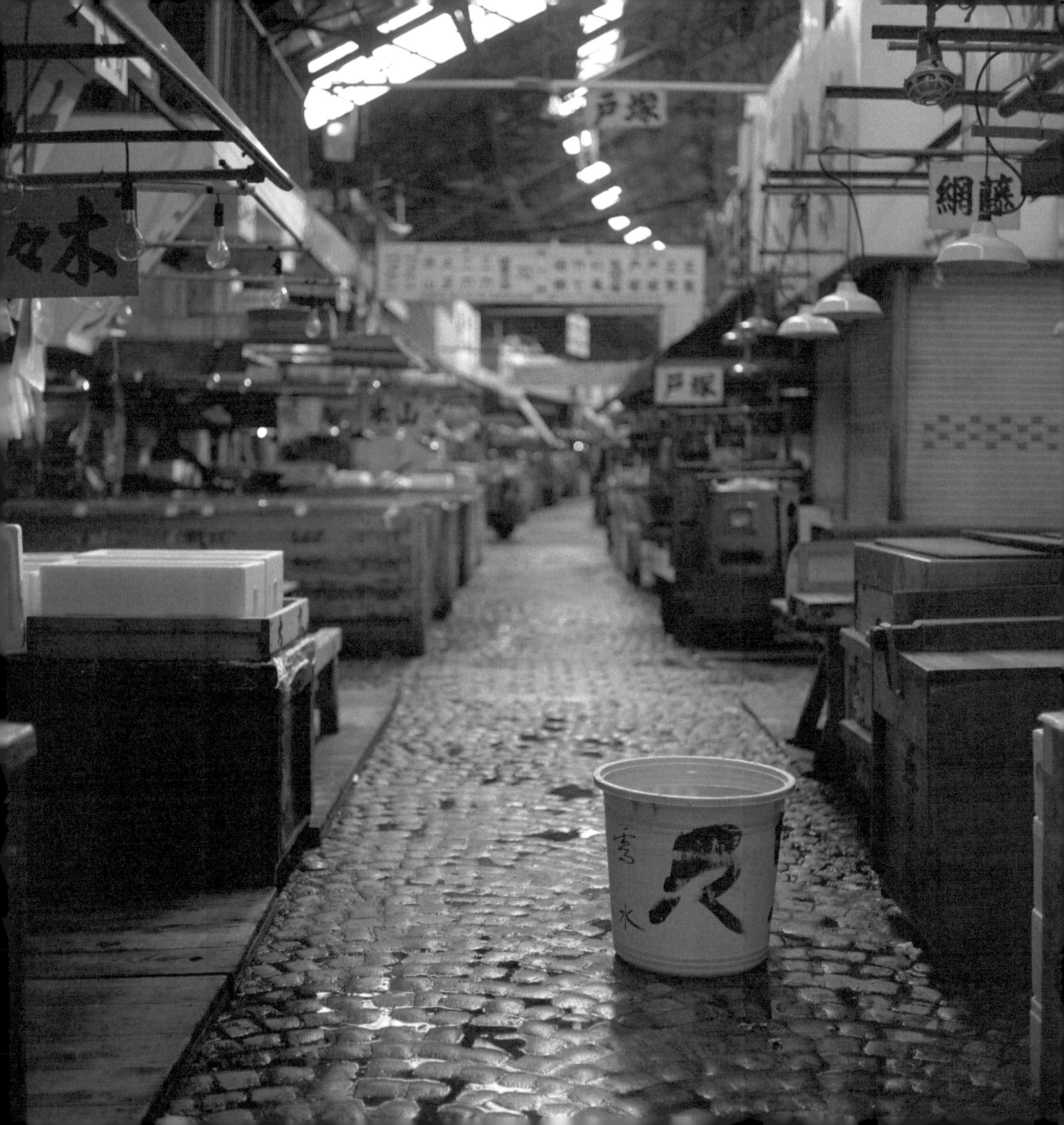

戸塚
網藤
々木
戸塚
雪
水

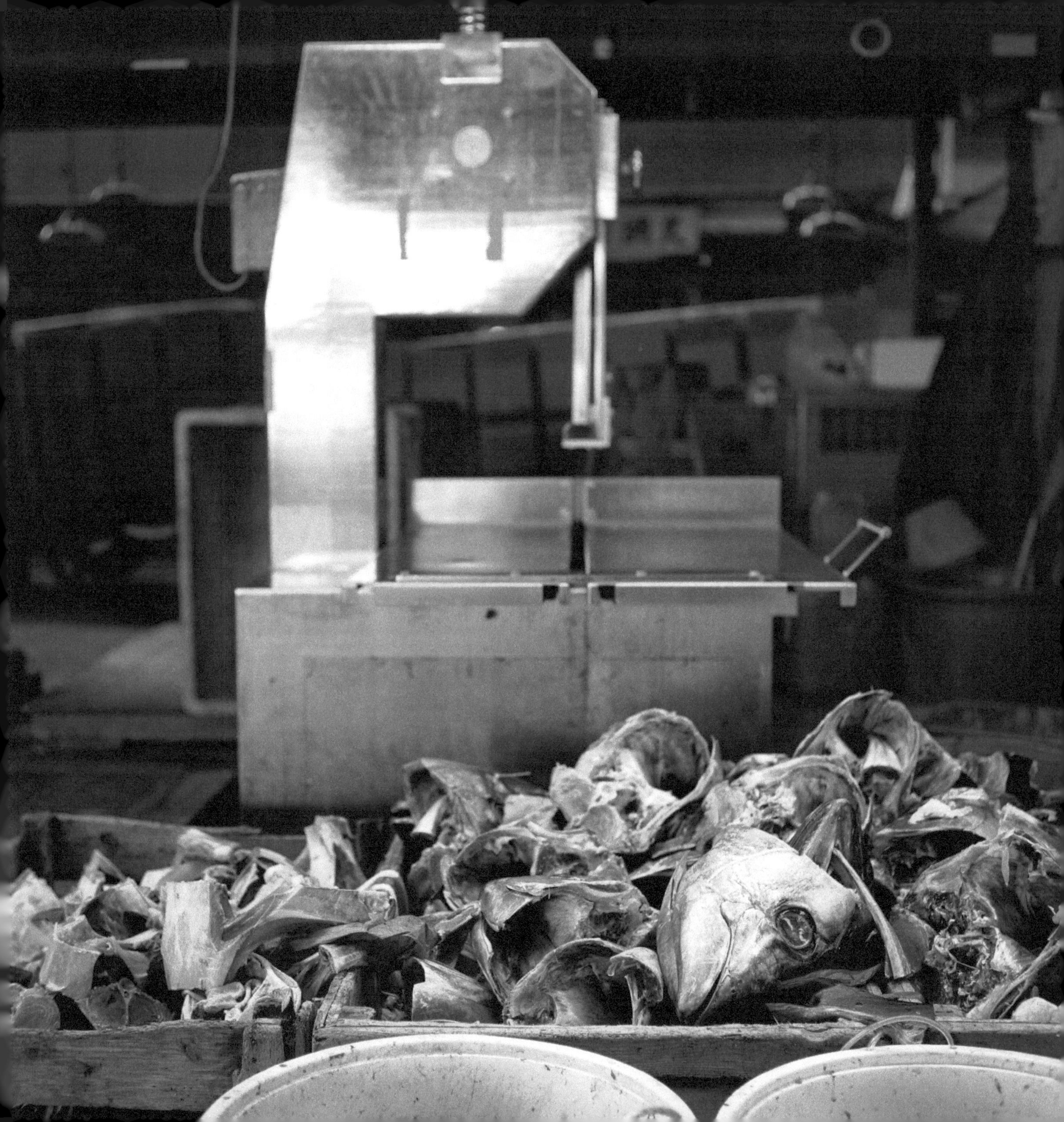

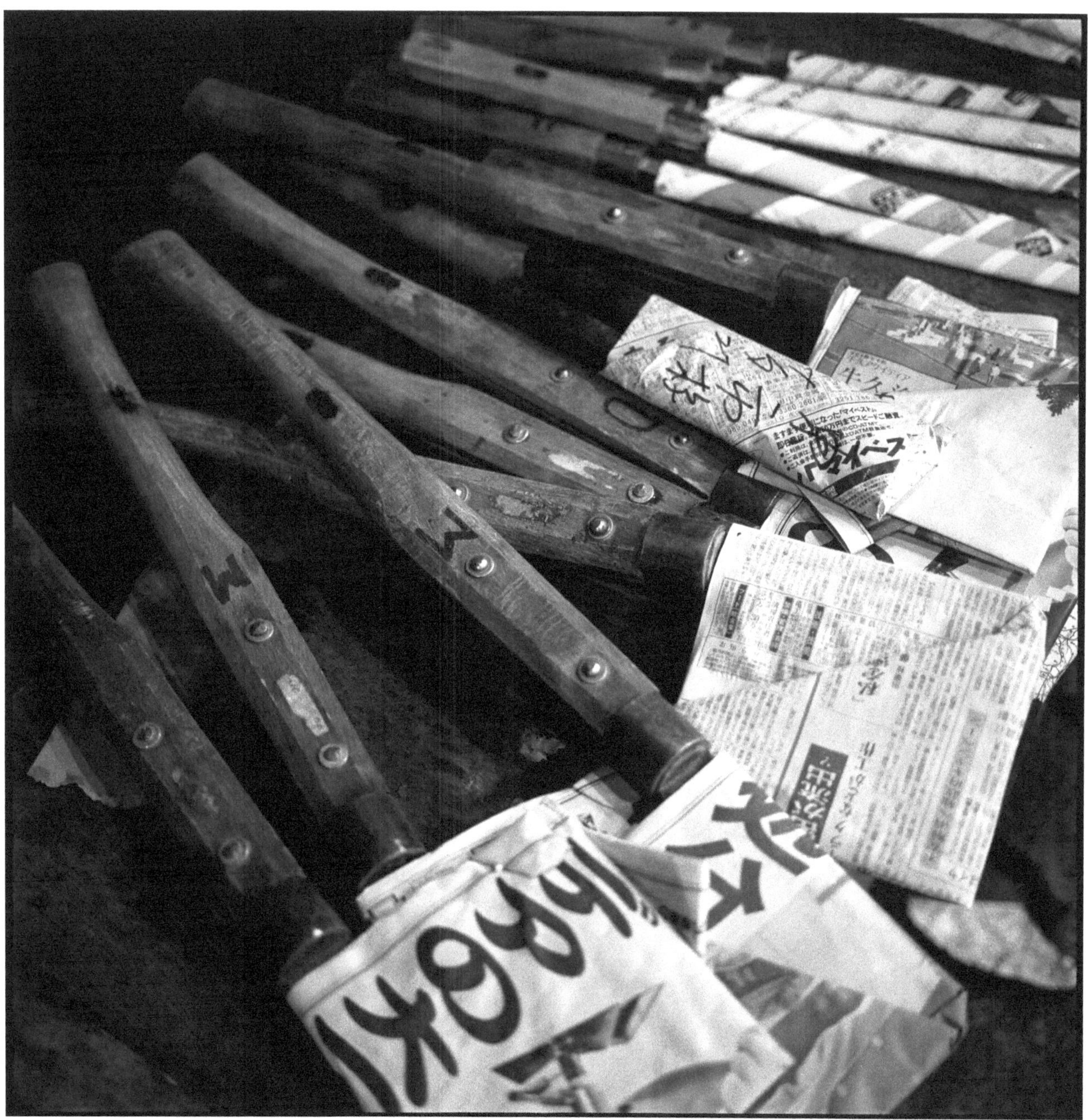

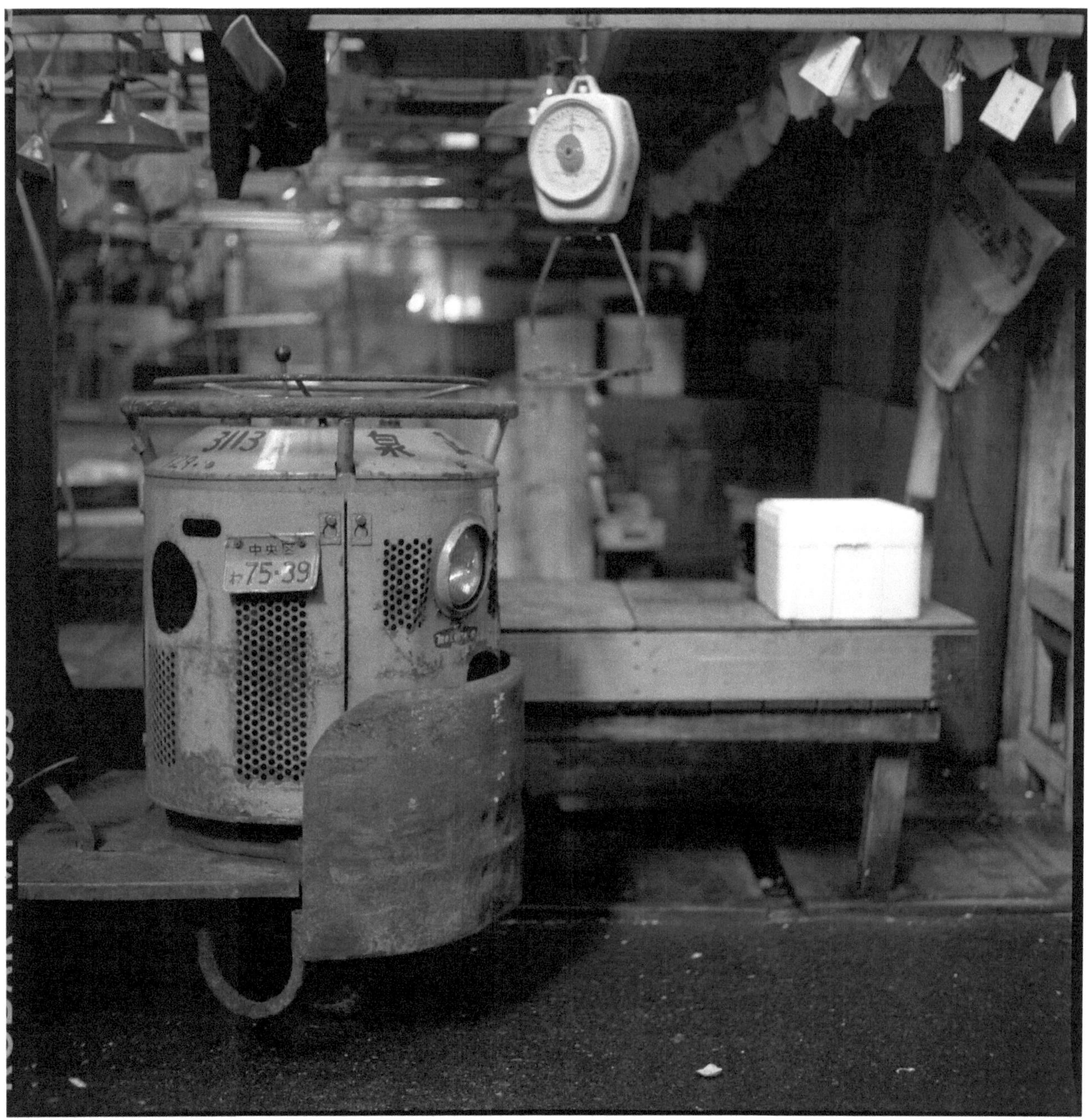

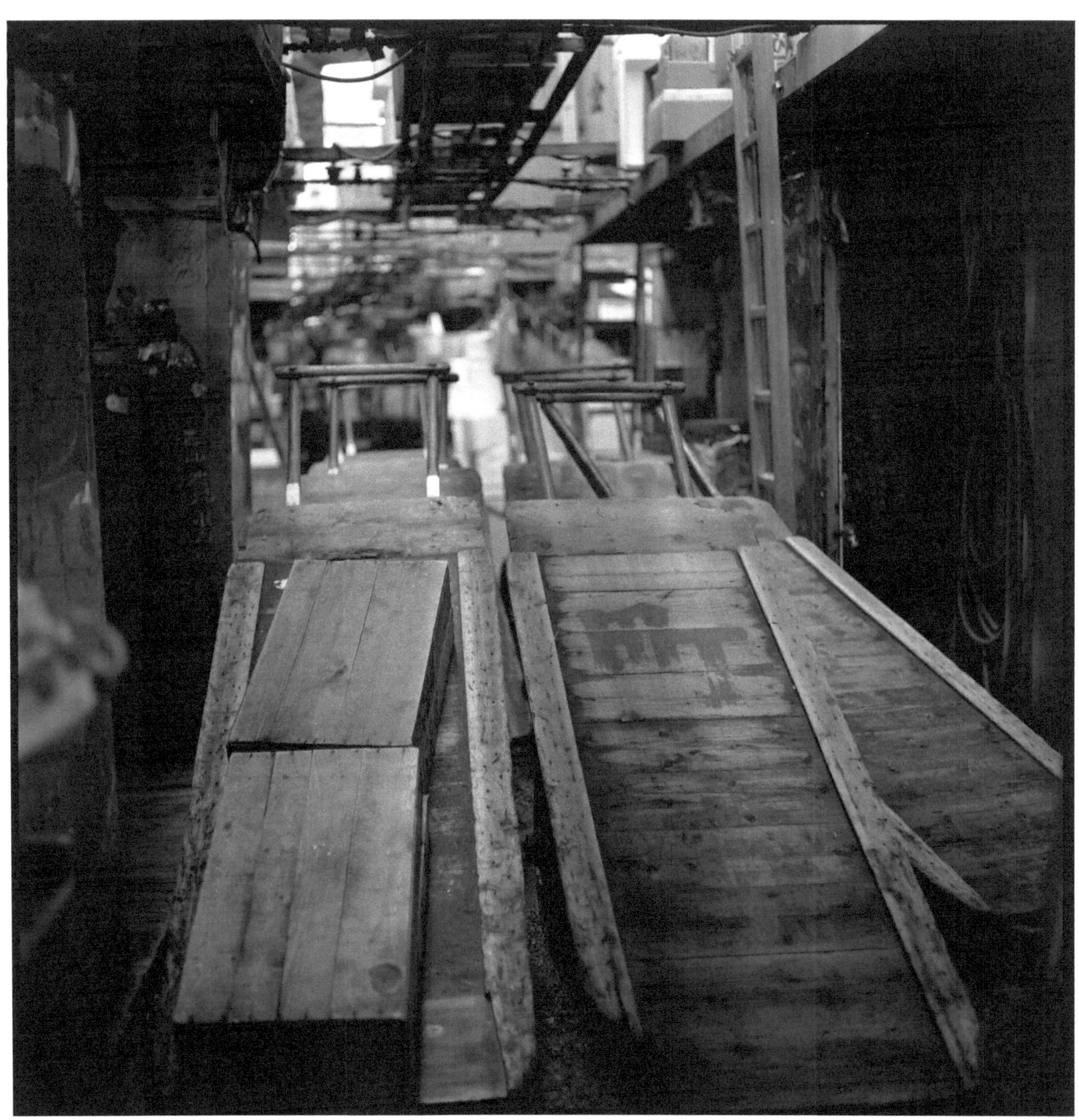

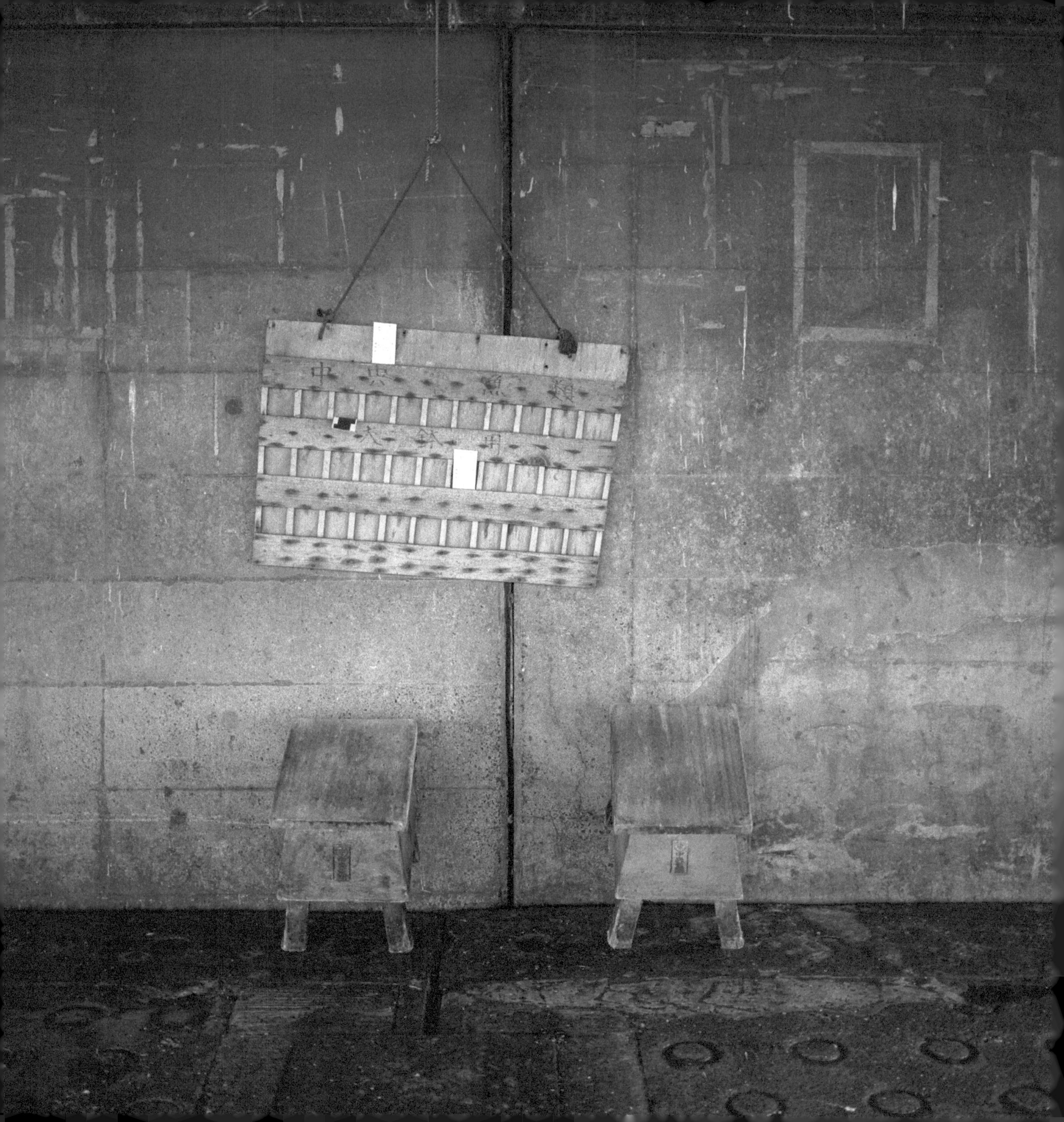

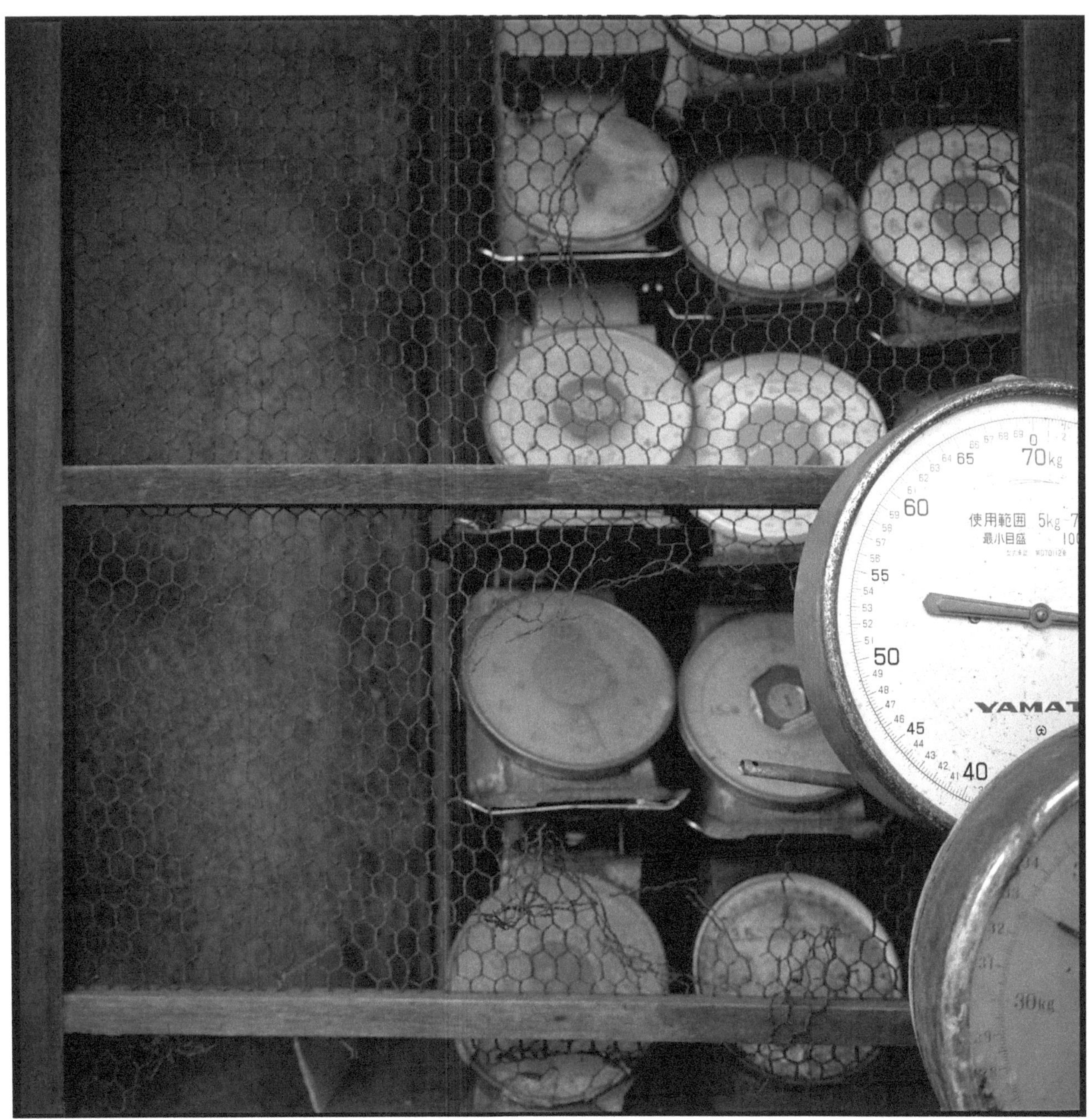
70kg
65
60
55
50
45
40
使用範囲 5kg
最小目盛 10
YAMAT
30kg